*Following
into Risky Obedience*

COLLECTED PRAYERS
OF WALTER BRUEGGEMANN

Acting in the Wake: Prayers for Justice

*Following into Risky Obedience: Prayers along the
    Journey*

Waiting in Gratitude: Prayers of Joy

Following
into Risky Obedience

Prayers
along the Journey

COLLECTED PRAYERS OF
WALTER BRUEGGEMANN, VOLUME 2

WALTER BRUEGGEMANN
WITH BARBARA DICK

WESTMINSTER
JOHN KNOX PRESS
LOUISVILLE · KENTUCKY

First edition
Published by Westminster John Knox Press
Louisville, Kentucky

23 24 25 26 27 28 29 30 31 32 —10 9 8 7 6 5 4 3 2 1

Book design by Drew Stevens
Cover design by Mary Ann Smith

Library of Congress Cataloging-in-Publication Data

Names: Brueggemann, Walter, author.
Title: Following into risky obedience : prayers along the journey / Walter
  Brueggemann ; with Barbara Dick.
Description: First edition. | Louisville, Kentucky : Westminster John Knox
  Press, [2023] | Series: Collected prayers of Walter Brueggemann ; volume
  2 | Summary: "A collection of prayers by noted Hebrew Bible scholar
  Walter Brueggemann that can be used in both public worship and private
  devotion"-- Provided by publisher.
Identifiers: LCCN 2023005968 (print) | LCCN 2023005969 (ebook) | ISBN
  9780664268275 (paperback) | ISBN 9781646983247 (ebook)
Subjects: LCSH: Bible Old Testament--Devotional literature. | Prayer. |
  Obedience.
Classification: LCC BS1151.55 .B784 2023 (print) | LCC BS1151.55 (ebook)
  | DDC 248.4--dc23/eng/20230707
LC record available at https://lccn.loc.gov/2023005968
LC ebook record available at https://lccn.loc.gov/2023005969

Most Westminster John Knox Press books are available at special quantity
discounts when purchased in bulk by corporations, organizations, and special-
interest groups. For more information, please e-mail SpecialSales@wjkbooks.com.

CONTENTS

ONE: PRAYERS *FOR* THE JOURNEY

TWO: PRAYERS *ON* THE JOURNEY

FOREWORD

Years ago, I was mentoring a pastor who thought she was making a routine home visit on an elderly couple. Good pastors know that no visit is routine. Wise ones are attentive to the opportunities that lie under the surface as pivotal moments in ministry.

After taking several sips of coffee and listening to some disjointed conversation, she quickly diagnosed that there was distress in the room. Every pastoral engagement has the potential to open closed doors. In this case, the ultimate source of these seniors' stress and quarreling *was behind a closed door*. Days earlier, the shelves in one of their closets had collapsed.

Like all of us, their lives were in the layers. Books, photos, treasured memories, and select heirlooms were now mixed with ordinary things like winter coats, a feather duster, and a vacuum cleaner. The disruption had metastasized from the closet and attached itself to every preexisting conflict in their relationship. They were angry, and they felt powerless and ashamed. Their well-ordered lives had turned to chaos. While everything in that small storage space was mentally and emotionally well inventoried, all of it was no longer accessible.

Hearing their distress, the young pastor put down her cup of coffee, rolled up her sleeves, and helped them in ways that they dared not ask. When she did, she learned something important about pastoral ministry. The couple not only reorganized a closet but were able to *reorder their lives*.

For many of us, Walter Brueggemann's prayers do what that young pastor did for the couple in their time of need. Many of us don't know where to begin. We find ourselves searching for vocabulary in a season of dislocation. We know "it's in there somewhere," but more often, the words we *yearn* to offer God seem inaccessible. In our weariness or frustration, our best and hardest expressions cost more energy that we can muster. Some of us are grieving. We are at a loss for words or there are no words. The structural shelving that once held our memories, treasures, and ordinary parts of our lives has collapsed, and this now impacts our energy, resolve, and relationships. Even if we could ask for help, we might not know what to ask for.

Brueggemann's prayers give new resources, new energy, and new possibility. He offers fresh vocabulary and images that serve as wonderful scaffolding for the life of faith. Who knew that a relationship with God could be so honest, so earnest, so painful, and so real? Brueggemann knows. He knows not just because he can quilt together nice words in an orderly way; he knows because he has wrestled these words out of himself, his experience, his faith, and his God.

The large theme under which these prayers are organized is journey. There are people who navigate their way through the world by maps and there are those who navigate by landmarks. This is both literally true *and true pedagogically.* Some anchor what we read or hear or see in a story or in an image, and others, in a linear outline; it's just how we are built.

Good preachers recognize the needs of both kinds of hearers and do their best to provide for both. The best teachers provide some linear direction *as well as* images as they recognize the needs of both kinds of learning styles. Good writers follow Jesus' sage wisdom and become disciples of the kingdom of heaven by bringing forth something old and new (Matt. 13:52). The best guides help us find our way on the journey by providing maps *and* landmarks and will not settle for one or the other.

Walter Brueggemann has shown once again that he is a trustworthy and seasoned guide for the journey. His vocabulary is rich and risky. Brueggemann understands that relationships need both *security* and *authenticity.* A relationship with God is not immune from those needs. Unlike many interpersonal relationships, *authenticity* does not jeopardize relationship with God, it *deepens* it. This takes practice and some unlearning and relearning. Giving voice and vocabulary to "what is in there" may uproot some of our assumptions and sensibilities about God. Once named and spoken, these things root us even deeper in the relationship *now that they have been said.*

Brueggemann's vocabulary always comes with freight. He helps us reimagine not only the dynamics of a relationship with God, but also the one with our neighbors. A neighbor and neighborliness are not just polite words in a lexicon. Neighbors are real, storied people with texture. Some of them are easy to love on the grounds of their need. Some of them might currently be enemies who are on the way to becoming neighbors. The change of status from enemies to neighbors requires a movement in the heart of the one praying. Enemies can and should be loved, but this transformation of status can't happen until hard truths are spoken to God. Once those truths are uttered, the one praying is *given* new resources for reimagining others. The dialogue with God about enemies, neighbors, and circumstances is the stuff of faith that challenges, tests, convicts, and summons us to something larger than ourselves.

Those familiar with Walter Brueggemann can easily cite by heart some of his memorable frameworks that can serve as maps. For the Psalms it is *orientation, disorientation, and reorientation*. For the culture it is *therapeutic, technological, military, consumerism*. For the contests between prophets and power brokers it is frameworks of *anxiety, control, monopoly, and truth to power*. For those needing a map, Brueggemann provides these as potential scripts for navigating his prayers.

Nonetheless, neither readers, nor God, nor the world, nor Brueggemann (!) is reducible to a framework—Brueggemann would *insist* on that. There are no simple formulas or shortcuts. Brueggemann is impatient with reductionism and every form of simplifying the hard complexities that go with a dynamic relationship with self, God, and others. Relationships require wrestling and negotiation. Sometimes those are contested, sometimes they are adversarial, and sometimes they come with unwelcome emotions that *feel adversarial*. Deep truths, long

kept at arm's length, once voiced, set inner and exter-
nal captives free. God's shoulders are large enough
(and God's ego is small enough) to take the hard
truths of our lives, truths about which we should not
bear false witness. This is some of the hard work of
being in relationship, but God demonstrates God's
own resolve in the person of Jesus. In him, God
reveals a willingness to meet us in the intersections
that are honest, raw, and human. Brueggemann's
prayers provide on-ramps to a new kind of relating
with God, self, and world.

The journey toward new relationships continues
as we navigate a new world. On behalf of a whole
church that has experienced its reality as collapsed,
that continues a turbulent journey toward reordered
lives and longs to find our voice and vocabulary, we
say to Walter Brueggemann "thank you" for your
prayers that help us orienteer along the way!

Marc Nelesen
September 2022

The theme for this selection of my prayers, *journey*, has been suggested by my editors. It is an excellent rubric for prayers, as the people of God, in both the Old and New Testaments, are indeed on a journey. They never travel alone but are always "on the way" with the God who summons and accompanies them. And because of that travel arrangement, they are always in conversation with that God, that is, they are always engaged in prayer. Sometimes that conversation is peaceable and companionable; very often it is one of vigorous contestation. Faith is indeed a journey, and the "conversation of the heart" is one of the fiercest constituent members of that journey.

Since God's initial summons to Abraham and Sarah (Gen. 12:1–3), Israel has been a people on the way in the Old Testament. According to the arc of that ancient tradition, Israel arrives in the land of promise, always the destination of the journey:

> Thus the LORD gave to Israel all the land that he swore to their ancestors that he would give them; and having taken possession of it, they settled

there. And the LORD gave them rest on every side just as he had sworn to their ancestors; not one of all their enemies had withstood them, for the LORD had given all their enemies into their hands. Not one of all the good promises that the LORD had made to the house of Israel had failed; all came to pass. (Josh. 21:43–45)

Along the way from the initial imperative to the final fulfillment, Israel faced many toils and snares. Along that way, Moses is the great exemplar of prayer who engages God in a series of contested conversations (Exod. 32:11–13; 33:12–23; Num. 14:13–19). Alongside Moses, his sister Miriam leads the women of Israel in anticipatory praise as Israel is on its way (Exod. 15:20–21). In turn, Moses echoes the Song of Miriam to affirm that the destination of the journey is not only the land of promise, but specifically the city of Jerusalem:

> You brought them in and planted them on the mountain of your own possession,
>> the place, O LORD, that you made your abode,
>> the sanctuary, O LORD, that your hands have established.
>
> *Exod. 15:17*

It is always Jerusalem: next year in Jerusalem!

It is important to understand (and to undertake) Israel's journey with the practice of prayer on the way. By way of inflection on this contested journey toward Jerusalem, we have the vigorous stormy lament prayers of Jeremiah, who, on behalf of Israel as well as for his own life, disputes with YHWH until, in the end, his prayers finish in unresolved travail (Jer. 11:18–12:6; 15:10–21; 17:14–18; 18:18–23; and 20:7–18). His prayers of course are uttered in Jerusalem, the contested destination of Israel's journey.

In the later tradition of the Old Testament, Israel reiterates, with sustained intentionality, the old tradition of journey as it begins again in exile (aka "wilderness"). Israel sets out on its belated journey under the exuberant imaginative impetus of the poet:

> For you shall go out in joy,
>   and be led back in peace;
> the mountains and the hills before you
>   shall burst into song,
>   and all the trees of the field shall clap their hands.
>   *Isa. 55:12*

As the Hebrew Bible ends (with its different ordering of books), Israel is under mandate from the Persian king, Cyrus, to complete its journey to Jerusalem. In the last verse of that Bible, the imperial edict is ground for both hope and action:

> Thus says King Cyrus of Persia: The LORD, the God of heaven, has given me all the kingdoms of the earth, and he has charged me to build him a house at Jerusalem, which is in Judah. Whoever is among you of all his people, may the LORD his God be with him! Let him go up. (2 Chr. 36:23)

As that Hebrew Bible ends, Israel is not yet returned to Jerusalem; but it is on its way there. That journey from exile to homecoming, a reperformance of the old tradition, is again marked by prayer, notably the long petitionary laments of Ezra 9 and Nehemiah 9. The journey is not ever simply a whim of travel. It is an engagement of faith that depends upon this interaction every step of the way. As Israel journeys, so it prays.

Many of my prayers in this collection were offered at the beginning of a seminary class. Most often in each case I took as a theme for prayer a text we would study that day in class. The collection will indicate that I ranged over much of the Old Testament as did my teaching. My effort was to create a pedagogical environment in which the text of the day could be seen as in some way immediately contemporary in its address to us in our study. On occasion this caused me to focus not on a text, but on a circumstance in our interpretive context for that day. With both text-based and context-based prayers, I wanted to bear witness to the claim that *a faith-based journey* is *a pray-practicing journey.*

When the early church reflected on the journey undertaken in the Old Testament, it was able to produce an inventory of those on the journey who had traveled "by faith." Thus it is attested that the faithful journey is toward the promise, even when they do not arrive at their destination:

> All of these died in faith without having received the promises, but from a distance they saw and greeted them. They confessed that they were strangers and foreigners on the earth, for people who speak in this way make it clear that they are seeking a homeland. If they had been thinking

of the land that they had left behind, they would have had opportunity to return. But as it is, they desire a better country, that is, a heavenly one. Therefore God is not ashamed to be called their God; indeed, he has prepared a city for them. (Heb. 11:13–16)

By the conclusion of that long recital of those on the journey, the text addresses the contemporary generation of the faithful that is to continue the journey of faith:

Yet all these, though they were commended for their faith, did not receive what was promised, since God has provided something better so that they would not, apart from us, be made perfect. (vv. 39–40)

Because the ones we remember "did not receive what was promised," the new generation must continue the journey. The urgency is to be "on the way." Such "being on the way" is the only chance that the older travelers on the journey should "be made perfect."

In the New Testament, the companions of Jesus are always "on the way," so much so that they came to be called a sect of "the Way" (Acts 24:14). Indeed Jesus' singular word of command whereby he recruits disciples is simply "Follow me" (Mark 1:17; 2:14; 8:34; 10:21). In issuing this command Jesus does not specify what will be entailed. The disciples learn that only as they travel with him. Once they are under way they come to understand that they are on their way to Jerusalem. That is, they are to leave the safer environs of rural Galilee to travel to the holy city where the leadership of the city has colluded with the officials of the Roman Empire. The journey will yield a high-risk alternative to imperial authority. The disciples do not know this as they begin their walk with him. Along the way, he instructs them (Mark 8:31; 9:30–32). He empowers them (Luke 9:1; 10:9, 17). He acknowledges their acute fear because of the high risk of contesting the claims of empire. Thus the "journey" is not a fanciful romantic outing. It is rather a mission to show forth an alternative governance that will, soon or late, here and there, displace the present rule of empire. That journey, when faithfully undertaken, will end in *faith on Good Friday* and *in hope on Easter Sunday*. It is no wonder that the journey of faith and hope is one of prayer. Without that sustaining conversation, the journey for any one of us could not continue. It is my hope that these prayers will be resources for that journey of faith and hope, with our destination of *an obedient Friday* and *a joyous Sunday*.

Walter Brueggemann
Columbia Theological Seminary

ONE

PRAYERS *FOR* THE JOURNEY

Holy God,
> Who has called this people for your own purposes,
> Who has placed us, even us, in places of calling,
We give you thanks for our faithful companions and
for your whole church catholic.
> We marvel at your patience with us.
> We marvel at your graciousness and
> > forgiveness toward us.
We pray for your spirit of renewal and power,
> > that our fears and our hopes may be submitted
> > > to your cross,
> > that we may experience the kinds of
> > > brokenness that are faithful to Jesus,
> > and that we may come to know in intimate
> > > ways that losing life is the way to find life.
We are, all of us, along with our brothers and sisters,
> > bewildered and anxious people.
We not only want to keep our lives;
> We want to keep our lives just as they are.
So come to us with your weak power, and
> your gentle abrasion,
> > even among us in our fearfulness.
We pray that you will keep your promise
of all things new.
> Give us courage for the costliness of your way
> of newness. Amen.

—October 15, 1976

HOLDING OTHERS
IN GOD'S PRESENCE

For the company of the faithful who have
     trusted in your promises and
     relied on the vision of your Torah,
For the brave men and women who have named
your name in hard places,
For faithful women and men this day,
For caring pastors and missionaries in places of
persecution and seduction,
For all the bishops of the church who struggle their
way to faithfulness,
For all the baptized who name your name,
 We make intercession this day.

We know that you do not leave yourself ever
without a witness.
 This is a hard time to witness,
 so we pray for the gift of your power,
      your wisdom, and
      your energy,
   that we may walk and not grow weary,
   that we may run and not faint.
There is no power except your word
   that lets us this day be whole. Amen.

—December 10, 1976

We scarcely take time to be holy;
   we pray on the run,
   come in late and leave early.

We scarcely take time to be human;
   we rush past the neighbor,
   and even miss ourselves.

We scarcely take time to notice
the goodness and beauty of your world.

We are so anxious, so overextended,
   so preoccupied, so propelled.

And you, amid our excessive engagement,
   you utter the day "Seven!"
   Six days to work . . .
   seventh to rest.

You, in your unanxious presence, take the day off.
Your angels spend the day reading Torah.
Your saints pause in gratitude and wonder.

Well, we are not yet angels, and scarcely saints.
      But "seven" us anyway.
   Invite us into your rest,
      that our restlessness may become
         penultimate in our lives.

We are indeed burdened, heavy laden,
      stretched thin.
And you, in the fleshed Nazareth guy,
      offer an easy yoke.
   Relieve us of yokes too heavy,
          of finance and obligation,
          of virtue and morality,
          of performance
             and all that causes us to
                miss "the Big Seven."

Be our rest . . .
   turn our violent restlessness,
   and make us new. Amen.

                —July 24, 2007, Columbia Theological Seminary
                              Continuing Education Event

DEPOSED FOLK
MADE NEIGHBORS

How strange you are, good God,
    that you gather those without rights or power, and
    transpose them into chosen people
        who carry your future in their midst.
How strange that in ancient Egypt
    you gathered displaced slaves and
    they became your chosen people.
How strange that Jesus came
    among distressed people and
    welcomed them as your kingdom carriers.
How strange that generous attentiveness
    to "the least" is as though it were done to you.
And now!
    We attend to many displaced peoples
        and
    we notice afresh displaced peoples in their own lands
        who have been displaced, devalued, and dismissed.
We confess before you and our neighbors
    that some of us have been preemptive
    in aggressive ways.
    We have been indifferent to the claims
    of sisters and brothers.
    We have been complicit in pretending
        we are legitimate possessors.
Thus we pray to you, strange God,
    do your strange work,
    and guide us in doing your strange work.

Do your good work that the world does not expect.
Do your work of being mother and father to orphans.
Do your work of being guardian and patron
    of disenfranchised peoples.
Do your work of restoring displaced peoples,
    of recovering devalued cultures,
    of giving back what has been lost
    but never relinquished.
You are the God who regards "the other"
as friend and neighbor.
    So bind us into your neighborhood.
    People your neighborhood with folk unlike us,
    and guide us as we learn to cherish and respect
        our neighbors
    who preceded us in the good land.
We pray your strange name as we await
        your strange work. Amen.

—December 12, 2015

We are among your people in these laden days,
             people summoned to passion,
             people too busy to notice,
                     too jaded to care.
So we pray for your busy, jaded, needful people,
among whom we stand this day:
We pray for pastors pressed to the wall in exhaustion,
       not themselves situated to receive the news
       for themselves.
We pray for congregations so set in habit,
       not able to be broken in on by your suffering.
We pray for the church,
             for the church closest here,
                 Presbyterians, and all the fearful anxiety
                     that sets us to war;
             for the Roman Catholic Church,
                 now so beset by scandal as to lose its way;
             for the troubled churches in warring societies,
                 so beset with violence as to be unable
                     to sing.
We pray for bishops and pastors and teachers and
elders and missioners,
    all those burdened by your people.
Come, crucified one; come, risen one; come, coming one,
    suffer us in and through Friday darkness into the
    glad light of your new life. Amen.

—March 26, 2002, Columbia Theological Seminary

Seventh day . . . day of sabbath rest!
   Six days you worked,
                  created,
                  made,
      and called it "good."
   "No man works like you!"

Seventh day of rest from all your work:
   "No woman rests like you,"
         free from all your deep productivity.
Give us rest this day
         from our endless productivity,
         from our thoughtless consumption,
         from our durable anxiety,
      that we may—along with you—rest with glad angels.

Seventh day—day of sabbath rest,
   but the day after Friday,
   the day you descended among the dead,
         working your groaning will for newness
            among our beloved dead.
   The day after a day of waiting and harrowing,
   the day between,
   the liminal day of new possibility.

Give us good sabbath rest.
Give us a day of waiting for you to break new.
Deliver us from "a nice weekend,"
    that we may rest your rest
    and wait your wait . . . for coming soon. Amen.

—January 19, 2008, January Adventure,
St. Simons Island

Here we are, fresh from Epiphany,
        fresh from stars and magi
            and gold,
            and frankincense,
            and myrrh . . .
We expected the glow toward the Gentiles to be
brighter.

Here we are, fresh from Epiphany,
  pulled in weariness back to the church
    with its programs and budgets
        and meetings and conflicts
        and needs and possibilities,
  pulled in anxiety toward a text
    that seems remote from us,
    with work about which we are not sure.

Here we are, led by no star,
  but by the burden of call, or
      the excitement of ministry, or
      the truth of the gospel.

Here we are . . .
  settle us for these days
    that pull between church and text
    or we may take this weary, anxious place
      as our proper habitat.

We pray for energy and courage
that, as we maximize our learnings,
we may be warned,
in a dream,
by a text,
through a colleague,
to return home another way,
led,
free,
ready . . . again. Amen.

—*January 7, 2008, Columbia Theological Seminary*
DMin Class

You are the God who has entered into chaos and
created an ordered world;
You are the God who has walked into the darkness
and created light,
   for light and dark are both alike to you.
You are the God who has presented yourself that
long Friday,
   submitting to death, letting death do its worst;
You are the God who in buoyancy has laughed the
Easter laugh,
   with the shredded shambles of death all around;
You are the God who in every season of failed power
and impotent death

makes all things new,
And we praise you!

While we pray to you,
   we know about the rampaging of death now on
      the loose among us;
   We know about wars that are not mere rumors,
                  violence and brutality in which
                  we are deeply implicated;
We know about the forgotten who are shoved aside
                  in the greedy race for "more";
We know about the intractable powers of injustice
            where death exhibits its endless vigor;
We know about the deep anxieties that beset us,
               frets about worth and success and
                  acceptance and winning;

We know about numbing down when we can
no longer bear the anxiety,
              of caring only for ourselves,
              and not noticing,
We know. But we are here today because all our
shabby knowing is penultimate.
And so we submit our small rendezvous with the
power of death
              to your ultimate rule of light,
              life, and joy.
We do not know how to get from here to there,
              from our moaning Fridays
              to your sturdy Sundays.
So we pray, and
   we sing, and
   we wait, and
   we obey, and
we listen . . . to stories of little girls brought to life again,
              of small children taken up in new life,
              to transformations and healings and
              reconciliations here and there . . .
              all signs . . . signs of your sure sovereignty.
You . . . God of life.
         We deny nothing of the data of death among us.
         But we submit that data to your liveliness.
         Come again, Easter God,
         Come again, here, among us.
         Come again in all your neighborhoods where
            the neighbors wait.
Remember what you have begun.

Finish your new creation that we may be,
        soon or late,
        now and always,
Lost in wonder, love, and praise. Amen.

—*April 25, 2002, Columbia Theological Seminary*

RENEWED FOR OBEDIENCE

We pray this day for all of your people
    who are gathered in your communities
    of faith and obedience.
We pray that you renew the church this day;
we pray that you reform the synagogue this day.
We pray for all faithful pastors and rabbis
    who name your name and seek your will.

These are hard days.
    These are trouble-filled days,
    and they may be dying days for some of your people.
        But there are many of your faithful witnesses
            who have not failed to name your name in
            dangerous places.
We thank you for your sovereign rule,
                for your faithful care, and
                for your promised presence.
We pray the promise you have made to your people —
    that we may be called to your presence and
    to your work —
    that it may be real and energizing among us and
    in our very bodies.
We pray in the strong tradition of Moses and
in the company of Jesus
    that we may enact your goodness in the world.
    Amen.

—November 17, 1976

For the mystery of the text,
and for the history of eyes to see
and ears to hear the text,
we give you thanks.

Our eyes are scaled
and our ears are uncircumcised
and we are children of another world.

We pray for the gift of perception.
We pray for energy and courage,
that we may not leave the text
until we wrench your blessing from it.

Amen.

—October 18, 1976

ON READING CHILDS ON
PENTATEUCHAL CANON

Scripting God,
we would rather have you face-to-face,
> direct,
> immediate,
> Spirit-filled,
> given in how it feels to us.
How odd, how old, how rigorous and starchy,
> how complex that you come
> in text, that
We face not you, but text,
> not you, but complex tradition,
> not you, but canonical "final form."
There we find you scripted,
> as doer of miracles,
> as giver of commands,
> as leader in wilderness,
> as source of life and object of praise.
More than that, we find ourselves scripted,
on the receiving end:
> with thanks for miracles,
> in obedience to commands,
> as followers in barren places,
> as recipient of life and voice of praise.
Scripted, only to discover that we are falsely scripted:
> into despair and denial,
> into self-sufficiency and greed,
> into fear and anxiety.

So we stand before the text and petition:
    rescript us,
    retext us new and whole,
    reread us to glad obedience to you,
    according to your deep, empaged word.
    Amen.

—February 21, 2002, Columbia Theological Seminary.
Brevard Childs (1923–2007) was a noted Old Testament
scholar and professor who has taught me a great deal
about the Bible.

UPON READING "THE PROBLEM OF THE HEXATEUCH"

We mumble along without thinking,
   I believe, we believe,
      we believe but it costs very little.
I believe in God the Father Almighty;
         we confess God has the whole world in his hands;
         we mumble about the Son;
         we finish with strong syllables about resurrection
                       and life everlasting,
      though even while we speak,
            we have thick anxiety
            about our immortality,
            deeper anxiety of the world
            beyond your good governance.
We talk so easily, confess so readily, doubt so intuitively.
We make a thin confession
   and all the while around us is a thick cloud of
      witnesses
      who themselves have confessed
            before Pharaoh,
            before emperors,
            in the presence of lions,
            confronting torturers
            and abusers;
These all died for their utterance.
And we confess readily, even glibly.

So we ask for gravitas
   and courage and daring energy,
To confess unashamed . . .
   and then live as have the bold ones
   who summoned faith beyond doubt,
   whom you gave life in the midst of death,
   we confess in the weary, daring name of Jesus.
   Amen.

   —*February 19, 2002, Columbia Theological Seminary*

(Lay School)

Your word is our command;
　　your command is our pleasure;
　　　　　　　　your pleasure is our vocation.
It is all clear and simple, and we mean well.
Except that our fear and our hope and our interest
　　are so powerful,
　　and so hidden . . . from us, not from you.
And so after we listen and resolve to obey,
　　we are left yet with the hard work,

　　　　　　　　　　　　connecting,
　　　　　　　　　　　　discerning,
　　　　　　　　　　　　deciding,
　　　　　　　　　　　　interpreting.
In the face of war, we confess you will us peacemakers;
In a world of greed, we confess you will us generous;
In a world of fear, we confess you will us bold and free;
Move us beyond rules,
　　and beyond bargains and calculations,
　　that our lives may be in sync with your large will,
　　that obedience may be our joy and our freedom,
　　　　the tone and shape of every day . . . all our days.
You who command us and power us in glad obedience,
　　receive our thankful obedience. Amen.

　　　　　—October 8, 2001, Columbia Theological Seminary

You are the God who sets all your creatures
into families.
You have set us into families . . . and we thank you:
    Some of us are only child,
    Some of us are oldest child,
    Some of us are youngest child,
    Some of us are in between,
    Some of us are best beloved child,
    Some of us are rejected, forgotten child.

All of us know the drama of alienation that goes on
and on;
Some of us know the hope of reconciliation;
All of us remember times when
      the birthright was stolen in the family,
      either by us or from us.

All of us remember being left empty-handed
      when the resources were passed out.
All of us are a mix of belonging and wound.
  And you are the God who calls us to reconciliation
     to be drawn into your orbit of forgiveness,
     and so to forgive as we have been forgiven.

Good God of all abused children,
    of all abandoned women,
    of all refugee families,

You remember
and you give us
the ministry of reconciliation.
So move by good spirit among us,
that in our wounded wrestling
we may finish well-blessed,
renamed,
yours,
and so fully ourselves. Amen.

—March 7, 2006

You . . . big, wondrous, sovereign, grand,
　　You with such great promises,
　　　　　　　　noble visions,
　　　　　　　　big ideas.
Then you call such as us to enact them,
　　and we, glad to be called, count the cost,
　　　　　　　　　　resist,
　　　　　　　　　　make excuses,
　　　　　　　　　　find alternatives.
You call . . . we answer . . . we resist, we finally go
. . . sometimes.
And you in the midst of our call,
　　　　　　turning kingdoms,
　　　　　　summoning empires,
　　　　　　managing floods,
To your glory and to our well-being.
Your big visions and our little calls.
We live in the mismatch
　　　　　　and on good days are grateful. Amen.

—*February 28, 2002, Columbia Theological Seminary*

(Exodus 1–15)

The story rings so true:
    we know about making bricks,
    about morality,
    and performance,
    and duty,
    and obligation,
    and expectation,
        and it leaves us weary.

We know about crying out and moaning;
    but we are the unanxious presence,
    so we must cover it over and move on.

But we know, we know about wounds
                and isolation,
                and bruises,
                and disappointments,
                and being unappreciated,
    so we do weep, even if in silence.

We know, in our best days,
    about singing and dancing,
    giving thanks and tambourines,
    and rhythm and freedom.

We know deep in our gut about departures
    but lack the courage,
    or the will,
    or the freedom.

So we line out the bricks,
                the cry,
                the dance . . . it is our story.

As we begin this day, we ask one thing . . .
only one thing:
    that you play your part in the story,
    that you be strong advocate,
                powerful agent,
                protective presence,
                giver of newness.

We will trail along after you in the story:
    we will weep all Friday
            and
    we will dance all Sunday.
We will, all this day, watch for you and listen for you.

We pray in some confidence,
    not completely sure. Amen.

　　　　—*October 22, 2008, Columbia Theological Seminary*
　　　　　　　　　　　　　　　DMin Day 3

(Exodus 1–15 Again)

It is only in your presence
    that we consider leaving.
Mostly we intend to stay:
    we intend to stay like Pharaoh,
    because we have it our way,
    there is no other place where it could be better.

    We intend to stay like the slaves,
    because we have cucumbers and onions to eat,
    and it is too scary to think to be elsewhere.

    We intend to stay like the midwives,
    but only till the contractions are timed,
    and we can slip away in the night . . .
                with the babies.

We intend to stay in lethargy,
             in fear,
             in despair.

And then you come,
   in a bush,
   in a voice,
   in a bulrush,
   in a miracle.
        You plant the seed of freedom,
                and leaving,
                and promise,
                and milk and honey.

We count the cost;
we measure the risk;
we ponder the loss,
and we say, "Not yet, not this time."

He said, "Let them go."
Later he said, "Follow me."
We have sugarplums of freedom dancing in our heads,
   but we wait . . . till next time,
              till a better day,
              till it is easier.

And we stay;
so what should we ask?
Your pardon for refusing? Amen.

     —October 23, 2008, Columbia Theological Seminary
                               DMin Day 4

Women singing,
children teeming with tambourines,
men dancing, in twos,
   in circles,
   with abandonment . . .
    A mass of exultant humanity,
     the dance of freedom,
     the silence broken,
     old quotas violated,
     heavy bricks abandoned.
Freedom . . . your gift inexplicable.
Beneath the joy . . . the churning of water,
    the gasping of horses,
    the floating of crowns from
    the heads of previous kings.
You . . . hidden but powerful,
You . . . transformative in fierceness,
You . . . towering in new sovereignty,
You . . . sung, danced, laughed,
You . . . given us only on women's lips,
    and frail witnesses,
    and church gossip, all taken as
    good news.
And that in a cut-and-paste world of electronic data,
    so impatient with gossip,
    so resistant to liberated,
     dancing women,
    so numbed to tambourines
    of newness.

And we listening,
    dance a little,
    doubt more,
    almost missing your new age,
    but grasping in the deep, churning water,
    up to our eyes, for hints of you.
    Amen.

    —*February 27, 2002, Columbia Theological Seminary*

(Exodus 19–24)

Our ancestors pledged,
    "Everything that the Lord has commanded,
        We will do."

But to our ears, "commanded" sounds harsh,
                and unbending,
                too much like obedience,
                or perhaps even coercion.

We would prefer a softer formulation,
    like "suggest,"
    or "propose,"
    or "negotiate,"
    or "accommodate,"
    or "consider."

But "command" allows no give . . . only take.

But then, we do know about command.
    We are under insatiable command in our economy,
        produce more,
        shop more,
        consume more,
        need more,
        desire more.

We are under inexhaustible command in our ministry,
    too many bosses,
    too many expectations,
    too many requirements.
Or deeper,
    We are under endless command to old ghosts,
        "do well,
        "be the best,
        "look neat,
        "and be polite,
        "and share" . . .
            endlessly!
But your commandments are deep and startling and
rigorous:
    LOVE YOU!
        With all we are and have,
        love you in your holiness and in our absence.

    LOVE NEIGHBOR,
        even the greedy ones,
        the predators,
        the muggers,
        the vulnerable.

    LOVE LIKE YOU LOVE YOURSELF.
        But we do not much love ourselves,
        though now so free to do that!

So we ponder "command," and you, and them, and us.
    We ponder and decide again
    to trust and obey,
    or to trust but not to obey,
    or to obey and not to trust,
    or to trust and obey,
    or to obey and trust.

We do know there is no other way.
    It is what our ancestors knew already at Sinai . . .
        no other way.
And now we know as well. Amen.

                    —*October 27, 2008, Columbia Theological Seminary*
                                              DMin Day 6

(Deuteronomy)

Through many toils and snares,
    we have already come.
    We have had some toils in our time together.
    We have had some snares along the way.
    (And we brought some snares with us when new
       arrived.)

In the midst of such impediments,
    We have listened a while
       to our ancient mothers and fathers.
    We have celebrated you,
       You who creates and recreates,
       You who delivers and feeds,
       You who commands and promises.

We have marched through their old testimony,
    And have arrived at the Jordan,
       the boundary of milk and honey,
       the border of promises fulfilled,
       the entry into seduction and transformation.

So we pause our life at the Jordan,
    partly in wonder,
    partly in fear and anxiety,
       not yet across,
          because the river is dark and cold,
          and we fear we will only tread water.

On our way back to ministry,
        back to real life,
Surprise us with your presence.
Give us eyes to reperceive your milk and honey
    right there.
Give us hands to do the work the new place requires.
Give us freedom and energy and courage
    for our newness that comes in obedience.
We pray in the name of the one who was baptized
                in the Jordan,
            faced Satan in the wilderness, and
            was fed by angels.
Send us your best angels for the journey. Amen.

—October 31, 2008, Columbia Theological Seminary
DMin Day 10

The proper mantras roll easily off our lips:
    grace and truth,
    justice and righteousness,
    mercy and compassion.
We can speak almost glibly and go from there.

And then we come to mother Hannah and
                brother David and
                son Solomon.
And find you quirky, cunning, hidden,
  not at all what we had in mind.

So we watch for traces of you,
    amid barren women,
    and ruthless generals,
    and dancing women,
    and killing brothers,
    and loss and grief and betrayal.
We read and then we mindlessly say,
    "The word of the Lord . . . thanks be to God."

We wish you were less quirky,
        less hidden,
        less cunning,
  more like our mantras,

except that our lives
    and the lives of those with whom we will minister
    are like that,
                barren,
                ruthless,
                dancing,
                killing,
                flowing with loss and grief and
                betrayal.

When we finish reading in stunned awareness,
        we sense anew
                that you are precisely the God for
                    whom we yearn,
                the one who can weave through our
                    troubled life,
                the one who calls to many toils,
                who sets many snares,
    but who stays till all the lights are out,
    and then endures even in the darkness.

You are God . . . we love you . . . and your scroll.
Give us eyes to see,
        ears to hear,
        hearts to notice
        and then to travel with you . . . light and
            darkness . . .
                presence and absence . . .
                with you. Amen.

— October 2, 2007, Old Testament Survey Class

You are the God who calls, stealthily and jarringly,
   You call the worlds into being,
   You call men and women into your church,
      of all ages, tongues, and races.
   You call such as us into ministry
      of word and sacrament.
And we variously respond and answer to your calling,
     • ready,
     • bewildered,
     • ambiguous,
     • fearful,
     • bold and confident . . .
Only to discover that
   You stand by those you call,
     faithful and steadfast,
        or
   You reject and dismiss and overthrow
     what we take as settled calls,
        or
   You push your called ones to new measures of
     risk and obedience.
In that matrix of your stirring,
   You call and we are called.
We ponder and trust and praise you,
   in the name of Jesus,
      who bids us come die with him. Amen.

    —*February 12, 2002, Columbia Theological Seminary*

God of grace and God of glory . . .
           God of glory . . .
           The words come easy to us,
           so familiar.
We sing, "Glory be to the Father, the Son, the Spirit."
We pray, "Thine is the kingdom, the power,
and the glory."
We sing and pray, because
                 we know the weight of your glory,
                 we trust the heaviness of your
                     sovereignty,
                 we affirm the deep tonnage of
                     your will,
                     and count on your glory,
                         sovereignty, will.
And then caught up short . . . as though we cannot
catch our breath,
                 to notice your vulnerability before
                     the powers,
                 you weak before your taunters,
                 you wretched in Friday emptiness,
                 you absent to the wonder points
                     when we so much crave your
                     presence.
The days become thin and the nights are longer,
                 your splendor dimmed to coldness,
                 we behold you in feebleness,
                     weakness that we sense in our
                     own bodies.

We hope for more and trust for more and expect more.
But now in Friday days,
    our great doxologies are at best hopeful whispers,
    our great affirmations muted to yearning,
    so we pray underneath the radar,
                come and save,
                come and show yourself,
                come soon in power.
Until then we wait in candor,
                but in candor, enough yet
                to obey, to trust, to hope.
                Come, come soon in glory.
                Amen.

    —*February 26, 2002, Columbia Theological Seminary*

You are the giver . . . endlessly, reliably, generously:
- You give dry land and regular light that the earth may prosper;
- You give your spirit of freedom in the slave camps, that the weary may dance;
- You give your spirit in the life of the church, moving us beyond weariness to boldness;
- You *gave and give* your only Son for the sake of the world and all its creatures;
- You give bread broken for new life in the world, wine poured out for reconciliation;
- You give yourself . . . fully and without reservation.

And we receive, sometimes gladly,
sometimes selfishly,
sometimes not noticing.

Beyond our receiving what you generously give,
we take and take and take and take,
until we violate your gifts and end in death.

All this day, let your giving outrun our need to take.
Give us gratitude to receive and trust and obey,
to *leave off the taking*, and settle for your good gifts.
Amen.

—March 12, 2002, Columbia Theological Seminary

We begin this study in a context where you
    have spoken to us in gracious, sovereign ways.
  You have spoken through prophets and apostles;
  You have spoken in Scripture that is always
             endlessly new among us;
  You have spoken among us by the
       stirring of your spirit;
  You have spoken to us and for us in
     Jesus Christ, your word fleshed.

And now we come to answers.
  We give you thanks
    for many mothers and many fathers
    who have responded to your utterance;
  We give you thanks
    for songs of exuberant praise, and
    for prayers of deep trust, and
    for poems of urgent imperative, and
    for shrill fits of rage addressed to you.

In and through our study,
     break our silences,
     hear us to freedom,
     receive us in our gratitude,
     and turn our bold words to thankful
       lives of faith and obedience.

We pray through the fleshed Word
who is your speech to us, and
our speech to you. Amen.

—September 5, 2002

(Psalm 145; 2 Corinthians 8:1–15)

Eternal God whose heart is goodness,
        whose primal gesture is giving,
        whose way is generosity,
        whose aim is the need of the world . . .

We begin the day in gratitude —
  we ponder your generosity,
  we name the needs that mark our life:
    need for care and for love,
    need for bread and for sustenance,
    need for purpose and meaning,
    need for forgiveness and for causes
        larger than ourselves;
  we name our needs . . . and notice in dazzlement . . .
    how you meet our needs:
      you overmatch our hungers
      you deal in majesty with our
          deep wants
  and we are grateful.

We confess before you a world of deep need:
      • saturated with violence
      • void of purpose
      • sparse on order
      • and lacking in justice.

We offer ourselves today as one of the links
        between your generosity
        and that needy world.

Through this day stretch our imagination,
                heal our fears,
                override our selfishness,
    that we may be—like Jesus—
                among those who make the world
                rich by our openness.

Move us beyond ourselves for the sake of this school
                and its body of support,
            for the sake of the church and
                its mission in the world,
            for the sake of the world that you
                love and care for.

Move us beyond ourselves—toward you and toward
neighbor—
    that we may become our true selves
                by giving ourselves away.

We pray in the name of Jesus, who,
        though he was rich,
        yet for our sakes became poor,
        so that by his poverty
        many might become rich. Amen.

—*April 2, 2003, Columbia Theological Seminary,*
Worship for the CTS Board of Directors

We confess you to be the God with a plan.
We celebrate your governance that presides
    over the rise and fall of nations,
    over the birthing and shattering of superpowers,
    over the coming and going of dominance and
       certitude.
You are the God who makes all else penultimate in
your splendor.
We are among those who affirm this large truth
    about your sovereign will, and
    our well-being according to
    your great destinations for us.
How odd, we admit in your presence,
    that for all our large theological slogans,
    we nonetheless are devoured in anxiety
       —as though we do not trust—
    devoured in anxiety
       about terror and disease and sneak attack,
       about our little deadlines and duties that
          vex our competence,
       about our most intimate relations that stay
          often unsettled.
We are a peculiar mix of
    large affirmation and
    close, intimate anxiety.
We suspect on many days that our anxiety is closer
to the truth than our
    confession.

So move among us with the gift of faith.
Match our faith to honesty.
Deliver us from denial about our true selves,
    and permit us trust midst doubt.
We pray in the name of your vexed, truth-telling
prophets. Amen.

—November 1, 2001, Columbia Theological Seminary

(First Day)

We come here from many places,
 at many speeds,
 with many burdens,
 with varied expectations and resolves.
We bring with us a lot from the folks:
 new, sweet-smelling babies,
 new waves of first love,
 new commitments of time and energy,
 old griefs resolved gracefully,
 new openness to radical newness,
 fresh courage for ambiguity.
Alongside, almost unable to leave,
 because of the grip of fear,
    two new cancer diagnoses,
    building programs underfunded,
    hurtful rumors around the choir,
 and in large scope,
    oceans of fear,
     of anxiety,
     of anger,
     of patriotism.
And in our midst wells up this scroll,
 a scroll dictated the first time in danger;
 a scroll shredded in royal rage;
 a scroll reproduced in danger;
 a scroll become canon;

a scroll become the live word of God,
"infallible lite,"
a word from the Lord midst our skittishness.
Draw us to the scroll,
and rescript us,
rescript us precisely for the hopes and
burdens of the folks.
Rescript us in freedom, in courage, in gratitude,
Rescript us for Friday risk,
for Sunday joy,
especially for Saturday waiting.
Rescript us, one more time. Amen.

—*October 22, 2001, Columbia Theological Seminary*

We remember better times,
    times of being smitten with you,
    infatuated,
    devoted,
    passionate . . . committed.

We acknowledge the cooling of our first love for you.
    We did not think it would happen,
    but it has,
        you being cranky too often,
        you being demanding too much,
        you being neglectful and inattentive to us.

But now, remote from you,
    we have a longing,
        a hint of desire for you . . .
    even a hope.

We hear you, faintly,
        inviting return.
    But we are not sure whether it is you calling,
        or our wishful thinking.

And then we ponder the price of return,
    more obedience on our part,
    greater attentiveness on our part,
    better policies on our part,
    embrace of costly justice
                and demanding mercy.

Your summons is steep;
    we yearn to be better connected,
    but pause, hesitate, linger,
        not ready to be seriously engaged.

We bid you—if you want us back—
    call more clearly,
    offer more generously,
    accept how we have become.

It is your move, before we move—
    needy as we are. Amen.

—January 7, 2008, Columbia Theological Seminary
DMin Class

(DMin Day 2)

You in your harshness, dismissing,
                                judging,
                                condemning,
                                devising evil . . .
You in your mercy, seeking,
                                willing,
                                wishing,
                                hoping,
                                reaching,
                                weeping.
You in your harshness and in your mercy,
You puzzle us,
You bewilder us,
You keep us off balance,
        You as you are . . .
        perhaps because of our fickleness,
                        are driven to extremes,
                        are pressed to craziness,
                        are impelled against your better self.
We in our fickleness, waywardness, hard-heartedness,
        we imagine we are in response,
        but we may be at the outset
        setting you into vertigo.
We in our empty failure . . . you in bewilderment,

we waiting for your better self . . .
    you here and there,
        past vertigo,
        back in balance, calling and waiting,
                softly and tenderly,
                wishing us home with you.
We yearning to hear your call, afraid to hear,
   because it means return
     through the mists of harshness,
     through the risk of mercy,
in a journey we fear and crave,
              want and dread,
              pledge and renege,
              start and hesitate,
              in all our double-mindedness.
So reach us with your single-mindedness,
   give us new, single hearts of flesh
   that pulse with praise and trust and obedience,
              with all our heart,
              with all our mind,
              with all our strength,
toward you, then our true selves.
    We pray in the single-minded name of Jesus.
    Amen.

      — October 23, 2001, Columbia Theological Seminary

(DMin Day 3)

We come to your presence haunted by an old question:
    The question is posed by your presence,
        for we would not ask it otherwise.
    The question is an old one, asked by our mothers
      and fathers forever.
    Haunted because we do not know . . . and
            we must know.
So now yet again, like all our predecessors,
    We ask again,
        Is there a balm . . . in Gilead or anywhere?
        Is there medicine for what ails us?
        Is there health care with you,
           so absent everywhere else?
        Is there a drug to deal with our infection?
        Is there a heavy dose for our pathology?
We ask, linger for your answer, but do not know.
We ask, then rush to lesser remedies,
                to quack physicians,
                to secret recipes,
                all the while thinking
                to heal ourselves.
But then back to you, still needing your answer.
    We suspect a "yes" from you,
    We ponder the way you healed old slaveries,
           the way you sent Jesus among the
              disabled,
           the way your Spirit has surged to
              heal.

We crave a "yes" from you and wait.
We wait . . . midst our disabilities of fear and anxiety;
We wait . . . aware of our pathologies of hate and
rage and greed;
We wait . . . knowing too well
our complicity in violence we need not see . . .
    We cut below that . . .
We wait in weariness, in doubt, in loneliness.
And we pray: say the word and we will be healed;
                say the word and our bodies will
                    move to joy;
                say the word and our body politic
                    will function again;
                say the word that you have fleshed in
                    Jesus;
                say the word . . . we will wait for
                    your healing "yes."
And while we wait, we will "yes" you
with our trusting obedience. Amen.

            —*October 23, 2001, Columbia Theological Seminary*

(DMin Day 5)

God of all our times:
> We have known since the day of our birth
> that our primal task is to grow to basic trust in you,
>> to rely on you in every circumstance,
>>> to know that you would return when you are away,
>>> to trust that in your absence you will soon be
>>>> present,
>>> to be assured that your silence bespeaks
>>>> attentiveness and not neglect,
>>> to know that in your abiding faithfulness,
>>>>> "all will be well and all will be well."

We do trust in you:
> we are named by your name,
> and bonded in your service.
> We are among those who sing your praise
> and who know of your deep faithfulness.

You, you, however, are not easy to trust:
> We pray against a closed sky,
>> Our hopes reduced to auto-suggestion;
>> Our petitions are more habit than hope;
>> Our intercessions are kindly gestures of
>>> well-being.

Sometimes more, many times not,
> because your silence and absence,
>> your indifference and tardiness are glaring
>> among us.

We are drawn to find lesser gods,
                    easier loyalties,
                    many forms of self-trust . . .
                    that do not fool even us.
On this Friday of remembered pain and
                    echoing deathliness,
We pray for new measures of passion,
            for fresh waves of resolve,
            for courage, energy, and freedom, to be
                our true selves . . .
            waiting in confidence,
            and while waiting, acting our life toward you
            in your ways of forgiving generosity.
We pray in the name of Jesus
            who trusted fully, and
            who is himself fully worthy of our trust.
            Amen.

— *October 26, 2001, Columbia Theological Seminary*

We are among your called.
   We have heard and answered your summons.
   You have addressed us in the deep
     places of our lives.
   In responsive obedience we testify,
    as we are able, to your truth as it
      concerns our common life.

We thank you for the call,
         for the burden of that call,
         for the risk that goes with it,
         for the joy of words given us
          by your growing Spirit, and
         for the newness that sometimes comes
         from your word.

We have indeed been in the counsel of your
   uttering Spirit,
   and so we know some truth to speak.

But we are, as well, filled with rich
     imagination of our own,
   And our imagination is sometimes
     matched and overmatched
         by our cowardice,
         by our readiness to please,
         by our quest for well-being.

We are, on most days, a hard mix
 of true prophet and wayward voice,
 a mix of your call to justice
  and our hope for shalom.

Here we are, as we are,
 mixed but faithful,
 compromised but committed,
 anxious but devoted to you.

Use us and our gifts for
 your newness that pushes beyond
 all that we can say or imagine.
 We are grateful for words given us;
 we are more grateful for your word fleshed
  among us. Amen.

—*October 29, 2004, Columbia Theological Seminary*

(DMin Day 6)

God of all truth, we give thanks for your faithful
utterance of reality.

 In your truthfulness, you have called the world
  "very good."

 In your truthfulness, you have promised, "I have
  loved you with an everlasting love."

 In your truthfulness, you have assured, "This is
  my beloved Son."

 In your truthfulness, you have voiced, "Fear not,
  I am with you."

 In your truthfulness, you have guaranteed
  that "Nothing shall separate us from
  your love in Jesus Christ."

It is by your truthfulness that we love.

And yet, we live in a world phony down deep
 in which we participate at a slant.

Ours is a seduced world,

 where we call evil good and good evil,

 where we put darkness for light and
  light for darkness,

 where we call bitter sweet and sweet bitter (Isa. 5:20),

 where we call war peace and peace war,

so that we rarely see the truth of the matter.

Give us courage
> to depart the pretend world of euphemism,
> to call things by their right name,
> to use things for their right use,
> to love our neighbor as you love us.
Overwhelm our fearful need to distort,
> that we may fall back into your truth-telling about us,
> that we may be tellers of truth and practitioners of truth.
We pray in the name of the One whom you have filled with "grace and truth." Amen.

— October 29, 2001, Columbia Theological Seminary

Like a father who has compassion
            on his children,
  so you have compassion on us,
    for you know how we are made.

We turn to you, good father God . . .
    We do so with wounded memories,
      for we recall our own history with you,
      seasons of harshness,
      words careless and emotive.
      We remember silences and alienation
            and rejection and blame.
      And know the distance of pain.

We also glimpse,
      in the hidden places
      of our common poetry,
      the breaks in your anger,
      the wistfulness that trumps anger,
      the yearning that opens in the midst of silence.

In these breaks and openness, we remember
  your good inclination,
      and so we come toward you again
      in confident hope.

We seek not your harshness, but your
  gentle beginning again.

We come to you, Father God, at the break of day
    and ask that you mother us all the day long.
    We are vulnerable and only your attentiveness
        will do;
    We are anxious and only your assurance will matter;
    We are needy and only your abundance will satisfy.

Let our prayer deeply move you.
Show us your mercy this day,
        that by nightfall,
                we may be dust-shaped in your image;
                we may be wounded ones
                    en route to newness;
                we may be turned by your mother-love
                                to boldness,
                                to freedom,
                                to joy.

(DMin Day 9)

You God, Lord and Sovereign,
You God, lover and partner,
   You are God of all our possibilities:
      You preside over
          all our comings and goings;
          all our wealth and all our poverty;
          all our sickness and all our health;
          all our despair and all our hope;
          all our living and all our dying,
             And we are grateful.
   You are God of all of our impossibilities:
      You have presided over the emancipations and
         healings of our mothers and fathers;
      You have presided over the wondrous transfor-
         mations in our own lives.
      You have and will preside over those parts of
         our lives that
         we imagine to be closed.
            And we are grateful.
So be your true self,
enacting the things impossible for us,

that we might yet be whole among
    the blind who see and
    the dead who are raised;
that we may yet witness your will for peace,
              your vision for justice,
              your vetoing all our killing fields.
At the outset of this day,
    we place our lives in your strong hands.
Before the end of this day,
    do newness among us in the very places where
              we are tired in fear,
              we are exhausted in guilt,
              we are spent in anxiety.
Make all things new, we pray in the new-making name of Jesus. Amen.

—November 1, 2001, Columbia Theological Seminary

(DMin Day 10; Last Day of Class)

We confess, when we ponder your large governance,
　　that our "chief end" is to
　　glorify you and enjoy you forever.
We confess that the purpose of our life,
　　　　　　　　　purposes twinned,
　　are your glory and our joy. That is our true end!
But when we come to the end of our work together, and
　　　　　　　　　the end of our text together,
It strikes us that we know less about
"ends" than we imagine.
　　We sing our explanatory doxologies,
　　We reiterate our concluding slogan that
　　　　"thine is the kingdom and the glory
　　　　　and the power."
　　We add our confident, loud "Amen"
　　to our best petitions.
But—truth to tell—
　　We cannot see the end;
　　when we see the end, we do not know its meaning . . .
　　　　　　　　whether termination or transition.
And so, like our many fathers and mothers always,
　　We trust where we cannot see,
　　　　eating what we are fed,
　　　　taking what of recognition we can muster,
　　　　restless and present
　　　　under a myriad of surveillances,

but finally ceding our end to you,
in our simple, final prayer:
>   Come, Lord Jesus.
>   Come among us,
>   Come to your church
>   in bewilderment,
>   Come to our state in its vexation,
>   Come to our world in its insomnia.
Grant us peace with justice,
>   peace with joy,
>   peace at the last,
>   peace on earth . . .
>   and glory to you in the highest. Amen.

—November 2, 2001, Columbia Theological Seminary

(On Reading 1 John 3)

We know how you are, enthroned at Sinai:
   Steadfast,
   Merciful,
   Gracious,
   Compassionate,
   Long-suffering,
   Forgiving.
We know how you are, embodied at Nazareth, so that
   The blind receive their sight,
   The lame walk,
   The lepers are cleansed,
   The deaf hear,
   The dead are raised,
   The poor have good news brought to them.
In your presence, we know how we are:
   Strange mixes of faithfulness and fickleness,
   Strange contradictions of good intention and feeble
      follow-through,
   Strange misgivings about self-love and neighbor love,
   Strange unsettlements about loving you and our
      many idols.
Given who you are
   and given who we are,
      we put ourselves down in this moment,
                     in your good promise,
That we will be like you:
   Like you in steadfastness,
   Like you in compassion,

Like you in transformative power,
Like you in forgiving capacity,
Like you and so unlike the way we are now.
We submit ourselves to your promise,
    Confident that you have not quit on us,
    that we are under way, by your goodness,
        To new selves,
        To our true selves,
        To us in your good image.
We thank you for your faithful power
    that outruns our timidity,
        for your long-term commitment to us
            while we are distracted from our true selves.
We fall back on you
    in an assurance of whom we may yet become by
        your mercy.
In the name of your bodied, transformative Son, we
thank you. Amen.

—April 23, 2012, Columbia Theological Seminary

You are the God who inhabits the scroll.
  We do not know how, but we do not doubt it.
  We trust enough to say . . .
    Glory to you, Lord Christ.
    Praise to you, Lord Christ.
    The word of the Lord, thanks be to God.
We say it even about the weird, objectionable parts
of the scroll,
  Partly by habit,
  Partly because we do not listen very much to
    what is read,
  Partly because we hunger after it
    And want a word addressed to us.
So we thank you for this radioactive scroll
  That has been set among us.
  For all of our criticism and our orthodoxy,
  It is not tamed or domesticated or made safe.
    Let it shatter, offend, and heal and transform.
For a minute tonight, position us in front of the scroll.
    Let it vex us and stir us and make us new.
We pray in the name of Jesus,
the sure child of the scroll. Amen.

—October 9, 2013, St. Timothy Episcopal Church

TWO

PRAYERS *ON* THE JOURNEY

We hold this text in our hand,
    Along with many texts.
    We read quickly, if at all.
    We read many texts quickly,
                Live fast,
                Too busy,
                On the surface.

When . . . or if . . . we look more closely,
    We are pulled back,
    We are pulled deep,
    We are pulled stunned,
    We are pulled old.

And when back and deep and stunned
and old enough,
    We enter the arena of our ancestors,
    Dead, but vibrant,
    Long gone, but present yet,
    Still trusting and resistant,
        defiant and pliable.

And yet further back and deeper and slower and
even older,
    Pressed to the bottom to find you there,
        You in holiness,
        You in fidelity,
        You in hiddenness,
        You in your irascible freedom.

You speak a while, and this text comes as
"word of God,"
     Word of you,
     Word of life.

For these days we pledge (as we are able)
         to slow our hurry,
         to deepen our surface,
         to linger beyond our business,
         to wait,
         to be addressed,
            and summoned,
            and made new.

You, page by page . . .
   holding our attention,
   knowing our names,
   willing our lives;
You, page by page by page. Amen.

        —October 20, 2008, Columbia Theological Seminary
                        DMin First Day

(Lay School)

We are your people . . .
   lingering in a remembered garden,
   looking to an awesome mountain,
   somewhere between garden and mountain,
     under promise, but doubtful;
     free but bewildered;
     fed but complaining
     . . . your people.
We remember the good garden of fruitfulness
     . . . and the whispering that misleads,
     the good food and the two trees,
     . . . one given, one banned;
     the good rivers and ample water,
     . . . all your will for life.
We anticipate the garden of good,
     when you will make all things new
     and whole.
And between that garden remembered
and that garden anticipated,
    in-between where we linger,
    We hear the rumble of the mountain,
     your awesome presence . . .
      about to speak . . . ten times to
      command, and
    we tremble . . . at your presence,
     tremble . . . at your holy command,
     tremble . . . at our new identity.

And from mountain, we set out to garden,
                    trembling,
                    resolved to be your faithful people,
                    elated to be your faithful people,
                        on our way in fear and trembling,
                        on our way in joy and newness,
to your new peaceableness. Amen.

      —October 1, 2001, Columbia Theological Seminary

We are the sandwich generation, looking both ways.
  We give you thanks for many grandparents
    who watched your violent deliverance,
    who bore witness to your power and
      steadfastness.
  We live in hope of many grandchildren,
    who yet will learn of your might and power,
    who yet will receive the world of justice and
      freedom from your hand.
And we, poised between
    grandparents who have witnessed and
    grandchildren who yet will hope,
we, poised between,
    are engaged in so much learning
                and unlearning,
    learning of your purpose beyond us,
    learning of your faithfulness against our fickleness,
    unlearning our trust in pharaoh,
    unlearning old habits of denial and despair,
    unlearning our deep love of brick quotas.
We, those before us, those after us,
    all coming to know you,
            to trust you,
            to obey you,
                you like whom there is no other,
                we praise you,
                you who makes distinctions
                and lets us be your people. Amen.

—March 7, 2002, Columbia Theological Seminary

We are your witnesses:
    We tell gladly
        what we have seen and heard,
        what we have remembered and been told,
        what we trust and on which
           we stake our lives.
    We tell gladly of your mighty rescues
        and your great gifts of justice and
        well-being.
    We tell joyously of your guarantees of creation,
        seedtime and harvest,
        day and night,
        cold and heat.
    We tell bravely that all is well and all is well
    and all will be well.
Caught up short in mid-doxology by the reality of
our lives:
    We know about loss and failure,
    We have heard tell about poverty and violence,
    We inhale daily war and rumors of war.
And so we bear witness as well,
    that we yearn for your assurance and find silence;
        we hope for your presence
           and meet dread absence;
        we watch for newness
           and notice the dry smell of what is old.

We tell what we know of you,
And in moments of daring praise, we tell more than
we ought,
> Ready to risk our truth-telling about you,
> > still unverified,
> > yet invisible,
> > but in trust and confidence and gratitude
> > for gifts you yet promise. Amen.

—November 14, 2001, Columbia Theological Seminary

We are too busy to sing;
we are too tired to say;
we are too hidden to speak;
we are too much multitasking
   to sound with a single voice,
   and the song withers at the back of our tongue.

When we pause an instant, in the depth of the night,
    there still wells up from the belly
    of our community
   old songs from our mothers,
   old cadences from our fathers,
   old defiances from our family,
   old visions from ancestors long ago.

We listen,
   and hear praise and hallelujah,
   and hear cries of bitter resentment,
   and hear accusations against your infidelity,
   and hear sighs over your long absence,
              and unbearable silence.

The songs of our community
        stream online below consciousness.

Here and there, we heed,
            we find voice,
            we move our lips
      and are caught afresh in praise,
                        and candor,
                        and anger,
                        and hope.

We break the busyness,
we escape the fatigue,
we risk beyond hiddenness,
we stop our multitasking
      and line out our lives toward you.

You listen . . . sometimes . . .
      and we are by our singing
                  made new,
                  made whole,
                  made yours. Amen.

—November 15, 2007, Old Testament Introduction Class

One time holy,
Two times holy
Three times holy,
   All cry, "Holy, holy, holy."
You . . . holy,
You . . . unutterable, dread-filled, beyond us . . .
       so unlike us.
We dare glimpse
  your presence:
  your holiness testifies to our uncleanness,
  your fierceness tells our apathy,
  your peaceableness notices our pugnacity,
  your generosity bespeaks our stinginess.
So unlike you, yet called by you,
        yet sent by you,
        yet authorized by you,
           to hard places,
           to tough times,
           to resistant circumstances.
Called . . . your instruments . . .
for all the neat, hard stuff . . .
    peace, mercy, compassion . . .
    all the hard stuff that ends in that unbearable
       FRIDAY!
Called to Friday as your instruments, and we are
dazzled, more dazzled than grateful. Amen.

      —October 9, 2001, Columbia Theological Seminary

We are mindful, O God,
that you have called us to the gospel,
and that you have set us in ministry
through our baptism.

We are mindful this day of all the faithful
men and women
who are called into your ministry.

We are mindful of our brothers and sisters in places of
temptation and seduction.

We are mindful this day of faithful
pastors and laypersons
who live under persecution for the gospel.

By and large, we live with ease and comfort
in complacency;
but we are not unaware of the scandal and the abrasion
that comes with your promise.

So we pray this day for the coming of your Spirit
that we may be found faithful,

that we may have power
and courage and energy,
that we may not lose
our vision of the gospel,
and that we may not flinch
from the suffering to which we are called.

For the sake of your promised kingdom.

Amen.

—October 13, 1976

In this deepest, most holy,
most demanding season of our faith,
    We are mindful of your self-giving
    that is without reserve.
And we are mindful of our need to receive
    from your self-giving . . . gift upon gift,
                  wonder upon wonder,
                  miracle upon miracle,
    gifts and wonders and miracles that you give
    in self-abandoning love,
    gifts and wonders and miracles that we receive,
                  sometimes casually,
                  sometimes gladly,
                  always in deep need.
So we thank you for your self-giving.
    We are, down deep, takers.
    Give us the freedom and grace to ponder
        your gift and your giving and You as giver,
        that we may be givers, in gladness,
                  in compassion,
                  in generosity.
Inconvenience our ordered lives by your gift.
Break the vicious cycles . . . and Easter us. Amen.

—March 26, 2002, Columbia Theological Seminary

For the promise of Sabbath to us,
   for the celebration of resurrection day,
   for the faithful watch your church keeps
   until your assured coming again,
      we give you thanks.

We give you thanks for the new day and the new
   week of work that you have set before us.

We begin it as strange mixtures.
We are, all of us, mixtures
   of excitement and weariness;
   of energy and anxiety.
We are all filled with fears that hold us back
   and hopes that drive us on.

In the midst of all our mixtures
   we do make faithful confession that you are God,
   that you are our only God,
   from everlasting to everlasting—to this day.

And so, in our faith and in our unfaith,
   in our readiness and in our fickleness,
   we submit ourselves to your safe care—
   knowing that you keep your promises
   and that you keep your children always
   according to your promises.

We make intercession this day
for all our colleagues around the world
who engage in theological study.

We pray that our work and study may be
a way through which the coming of your Spirit
is real and powerful to your church.

We pray according to our faith
in Jesus of Nazareth. Amen.

—October 25, 1976

You are the voice we can scarcely hear
because you speak to us about dying and suffering, and
we are addressed by so many voices that have to do with
   power and competence and success.

We do know that you are the voice that gives life,
that you are the voice that opens futures to people
who are hopeless.
We are on some days a part of a hopeless people,
because the other voices eat at our hearts,
and we are immobilized; we become deaf.

So we pray for new ears.

We pray that your voice may be more audible to us,
that we may be able to sort out the death-giving voice
from your life-giving word among us.

We pray in the name of Jesus, through whom you
have spoken in such inscrutable ways.

Amen.

—October 1, 1976

A DAY OF
CONTINUING EDUCATION

Great, good God who orders the world,
            who wills good for all creatures,
            who counts and treasures the
                hairs on our heads,
            who watches over until the world
                becomes "very good,"
Great, good God . . . our God!
        We begin the day with you,
        set afloat in an ocean of anxiety all around,
                in a fever of war and killing,
                in a swoon of arrogance with
                    overflowing power and wealth,
                in a bewilderment of fear and hate.
While we keep afloat . . . this little company,
We join the great company of believers,
                in naming your name,
                in pondering your will,
                in trusting your promises.
Through our work together this day cause us . . .
according to your purposes . . .

to be your serpents, wise in the ways of the world,
     your doves, innocent as the lamb
        that was slain,
     your people in praise and joy and obedience,
     your people, unfevered by anxiety,
                 unmarked by hate,
                 unimpeded by killing greed,
     your people in glad obedience,
     your people. Amen.

—*January 31, 2002, Columbia Theological Seminary*

You hover in the midst of our posturing:
  We seek control and guess at your will.
  We take new initiatives,
    and imagine them to be your intent.
  We hold on to old arrangements,
    and are very sure they are your arrangements.
We find ourselves often, too often,
    exactly at the break point,
                between what has been and
                what will be.
  Some of us tilt to what was . . . but do not know.
  Some of us tilt to what will be . . . but do not know.
And all the while, you stay hidden and powerful,
                unseen but decisive,
                mute but engaged.
We ask, amid your hidden, unseen muteness,
    for courage to live our lives,
    for freedom to relinquish what was,
    for nerve to receive what will be, finally
    for confidence in you, to trust,
                that all our postures are held
                firmly in your good grace.
                And we are thankful. Amen.

—*March 7, 2002, Columbia Theological Seminary*

At our best, we are able to say gladly:
    The Lord gives,
    The Lord takes away,
    Blessed be the name of the Lord.
At our best, we are ready and able to entrust our life
to you,
    in sickness and in health,
    in riches and in poverty.
We gladly affirm that you give . . .
    far more abundantly than we can ask or imagine . . .
      material comforts in our privilege,
      meaningful work,
      a sense of well-being and moral coherence.
    And we thank you.
We gladly affirm that you take away . . .
    But then we are sobered when it really happens,
      not as easy or comfortable as we had imagined.
    You take away and the loss is beyond what we
      had trusted.
        We ponder the loss
          of moths that consume,
          of rust that erodes,
          of thieves that steal in violence.
We are bewildered, anxious, angered,
    at you,
    at whoever . . . indignant and graceless.

So we ask for freedom to receive from you and
relinquish to you.
We ask for faith to trust you when you give and
when you take away.
We ask for a sense of well-being not grounded in
what we covet.
We ask for imagination to resituate our lives in your life,
     a life of death and newness,
        of absence and surprising presence,
        of threat and joy.
And we will as your people, as we are able,
     be on your way in confidence.
We pray in the name of the one who emptied himself,
        and whom you exalted in wonder and in
        Easter joy. Amen.

— September 25, 2001, Columbia Theological Seminary

We know all about the darkness,
>   walking in it,
>   dreading it,
>   seeking frantically to overcome it . . .
>>   with security lights,
>>   and with security weapons.
But left in darkness . . . until
>>   your light comes to overwhelm the darkness
>>   and refuses to be contained by the darkness.
We know about light coming:
- coming day by day in your good creation, morning by morning,
- coming in the gift of your Torah that is a light unto our path,
- coming in Jesus of Nazareth who has defeated the powers of darkness,
- coming, but left waiting,
>>>   waiting for your light,
>>>   while the darkness yet pervades,
>>>   your light promised, but not yet given,
>>>   your light sure, but not on our terms.
Your light, because light and dark are both alike to you.
Be our light in these dark days,
>   and let us walk by faith where we cannot yet see.
>   Amen.

—October 11, 2001, Columbia Theological Seminary

We belong, many of us, to that company nurtured in
    a simple, direct faith:

    We could readily recall "awesome deeds,"
        not least Easter resurrection,
        water to wine,
        bread for five thousand, and
        lepers healed by the power of God.

    We could also recognize
        "divine anger"
           given in parental disappointment,
        a sense of sin and shame,
        a readiness to bow in contrition,
           and traces of new grace.

We embraced that faith in essence,
    and then became sophisticated,
    and now know too much to crave miracle.

We became sophisticated
    and now cherish our own autonomy, come of age.

We arrive with some embarrassment at
    "awesome deeds"
    and stand at some distance from "divine anger."

Being on our own in a cold world, in unguarded
moments nonetheless . . .

> We sense our role as orphan
>   and yearn for you as "Father";

> We wish so much to say, "You are our father";

> We go behind sophistication
>   and our unprecedented affluence
>   and want welcome home, embrace,
>   divine presence, and peace;

> We want and hope, not fully convinced,
>   but alive to our true and deep need.

And so we pray as sons and daughters
>   to our Father who is in heaven. Amen.

—May 17, 2005

We turn to you,
> because we have exhausted all our other allies.
> We come to you in need,
>> in expectation,
>> in a bit of self-pity.
> Because we are honest does not mean that
> we are excessively paranoid.

But we do notice that because of our call,
> We are regularly in high-risk places,
>> places of dispute and conflict
>>> with those who do not fight fair.

If we are blessed by you,
> we would receive from you some affirmation,
>>> some vindication,
>>> some tilt toward us
>>>> and against the
>>>> troublemakers.

If we are honest, we feel caught on your behalf,
> weary, without visible support.

In our need,
> your strictness does not help.
>> Your demands are unending,
>> your requirements are insatiable,
>> your expectations are beyond our capacity.

So we ask for a sign of presence,
    a gesture of solidarity,
    a gift of deliverance.
We do trust you.
  Out of your "do not fear,"
    we pledge courage;
  out of your word to us "at the close of the age,"
    we vow staying at it.
We will, for now, stay at it
  in courage and freedom,
  in hope,
  with the buoyancy of your Easter guy. Amen.

        —*January 10, 2008, Columbia Theological Seminary*
                                    DMin Class

Where you lead us, we will follow:
He called and said, "Follow me."
   We are his followers, baptized into his company.
He called us . . . to follow him into a world of fear
and threat and anger,
                   To follow in obedience,
                   To follow in gladness,
                   To follow in buoyant confidence.
We are sometimes his willing followers, ready to go.
We are sometimes his reluctant followers, slow to
get under way.
We are sometimes stubborn nonfollowers,
   preferring other paths
      of our own contrivance.
So now, in your presence, and in the presence of our
sisters and brothers,
   We ponder again our vocation,
                   our baptism,
                   our discipleship,
                   our way in the world.
We know ourselves, in your presence, to be carriers
of your way
   Of mercy, compassion, and justice,
      way out beyond our comfort zones.
   We are practitioners of your goodness,
                      your generosity,
                      your hospitality.

In this hour of baptismal reflection,
     revive our new identity in Jesus,
     revive our pledge of fresh obedience,
     revive our passion
                         for our world of need,
                                   of violence,
                                   of poverty.
Look on this old, tired world with your mercy, and
     make new,
     make things new for us,
     make things new for those who are sick or who
          grieve,
     make things new for those with power and wealth,
          and for those without power and wealth,
     make things new on this very day.
Hear our pledge that we will walk into that world
with you,
     So that the world may breathe easy again,
          with thanks and joy and peace. Amen.

—*February 22, 2015, Mount Auburn Presbyterian Church,*
Cincinnati, Ohio

We do not know what we ask,
    when we pray for newness.

We do not know the route
    from old and failed
    to new and fresh.

We do not know what it costs you . . .
    at the bottom of your holiness . . .
    to reach where grace may abound.

    We do not know,
    but we ask anyway:
        we ask out of our leanness and despair,
        we ask out of our mix of hope and hopelessness,
        we ask out of our memory of your ancient
            miracles . . .
                another exodus . . .
                another Easter . . .
                another creation.

We ask for our own bodies in their exhaustion.
We ask for the body of the church
    that we say is "the body of Christ."
We ask for the body politic.

    We believe . . . on a good day . . .
                in the resurrection of the body.

So look upon this body frayed and in need,
   our own,
   that of the church,
   that of our wounded society.
Give newness . . .
Break old patterns that we cherish.
Revive us . . . again . . .

You awesome power for life. Amen.

—*October 28, 2008, Columbia Theological Seminary*
DMin Day 7

(On Reading Psalm 74)

We had it all figured out.
We had saved enough for many rainy days.
We managed by our know-how and our piety and
our morality
    to maintain an ordered life in an ordered world.
We were sure enough
  in our whiteness,
  in our Americanism,
  in our maleness . . . some of us,
  in our undoubted chosenness.
And then puff!
  The world has become strange and alien to us;
  What we thought was safe is not;
  We crave old better ways,
  Old truth,
  Old certitude,
  Old assurance,
  Old ways church.
And then puff!
  Comes the threat of new folks with their passion
    and ideology,
  Comes the threat of dangerous ideas,
  Comes the requirement of new mystifying
    technology,
  Comes the fresh stirring of hate and fear.

  Given all of that so real for us,

We in faith still say "Yet!"
   Yet you!
   Yet you as king of the earth,
   Yet you as the one who crushes evil,
   Yet you who sends rain and drought,
   Yet you, Lord of sun and moon.

We deny nothing that is in front of us;
Nevertheless, we turn to you,
           we pray to you,
           we petition you.

We do that in our vulnerability,
           in complete confidence. Amen.

God of Sarah who gave an impossible baby;
God of Mary who gave another impossible baby;
God of Israel who freed slaves against the
       long odds of Pharaoh;
God of Jesus who raised him from the
 dead and defied the powers of death;
God of the church who has done the impossible
 work of forgiveness and reconciliation . . .

We situate our lives around what the world
       calls possible:
 We accept violent definitions of peace;
 we accept grudging notions of justice;
 we settle for shabby notions of health.

And then, in crunch time, we hope for more:
 We hope, against the violence, for peace;
 we hope, against the grudging, for justice;
 we hope, against the shabbiness, for health.

We pray in need, but we also pray in hope
  that you will . . . yet again . . .
  outmuscle the powers of death.

Give us patience to receive what you give;
accept our impatience for wanting all that you can give;
notice us, attend to us,
   do your impossibility . . .
         make all things new,
            in our world,
            in the church,
            even in our bodies.
We pray in the healing name of Jesus. Amen.

   —*November 17, 2006, Columbia Theological Seminary,*
                              for Carolyn Wilhelm

First it was milk from mother,
 and then puree and carrots and spinach,
 then finally to meat,
  and when we dared,
  wine and beer and gin.
From the outset we have been eaters and drinkers,
 eaters who have been given food,
 drinkers who have taken it all for granted.
We have been such entitled eaters and drinkers
 that eventually we managed our own food supply,
     bought the bakery,
     owned the dairy,
     controlled the brewery.
So we come to the day full, and then
 You haunt us by a small room . . . twelve guests
  . . . one unwelcome,
 and your strange bread of obedience,
  discipleship, and affliction . . .
 always broken, strange wine,
  poured out as new covenant . . .
 along with your unclear words, something about
     "This is me . . . my body . . . my blood,
     blessed, broken, poured out, given,"
      not on our terms!
Our hungers are Thursday deep for food we do not
produce.

Feed us with broken, poured-out you,
so that we do not hunger our way
            to the dread of Friday. Amen.

   —March 28, 2002, Columbia Theological Seminary

The narrative reports that Jesus fed five thousand people and had twelve baskets of bread left over (Mark 6:30–44). Then he fed four thousand people and had seven baskets left over (8:1–10). But even after all of that, his disciples had anxiety about bread. Their anxiety seems a misfit with the abundance of bread. In response to their anxiety, Jesus asks his disciples, "Why are you still talking about having no bread?" (8:17). Perhaps he is astonished about their obtuseness. More likely he is irritated that they do not trust his abundance.

I

Either way, we still talk about bread:
 It is the staff of life;
 It is the irreducible sustainer of life;
 It is the meeting place when
 "we break bread together."
  It must be given, and received,
  broken and shared, and chewed.
  It may be buttered and sliced and toasted.
   Life depends on it!
We still talk about having no bread, or not enough
 or bread that is organic or gluten free.

II

The first time we talked about no bread
was back with father Abraham
and mother Sarah (Gen. 12:10) . . . in a famine.
    We knew what to do.
    We went to Egypt, and we ate the bread of Pharaoh;
        It turned out to be a hazardous way to secure
            bread.
The second time we talked about no bread was after
we left Pharaoh's Egypt (Exod. 16:2–5).
    Pharaoh had plenty of bread. But we entered
        wilderness where there was no bread.
        We complained; Moses was irritated with us.
                    But God gave bread.
    It came down from heaven;
        we were surprised and did not recognize it.
        We said, "What is it [*man-hu*]?"
        And it was named "manna."
        We wondered about it;
        it turned out to be Wonder Bread
        sent from heaven above.
    There was enough for all;
    each one took what was needed.
        But we could not store up any surplus.
        Provision was made for sabbath rest;
        we had no need to gather bread on
                    sabbath . . . real rest!!
But then "manna ceased" (Josh. 5:12).
    We knew bread from heaven, but now bread from
        the earth, by soil and labor and agriculture
        and plowing and planting and harvesting and
            storing.

Our bread became quarrelsome,
>   Because some had big granaries
>   and some had nothing;
>   children starved, and
>   men fought over bread, and
>   mothers cried about the lack
>   for their children.
Later on, the poet chided us (Isa. 55:1–2),
> because we had signed on for bread from the empire,
> from the military, from the banks,
> from the greed system.
The poet wondered why we labored for such bread
>   that did not satisfy or nourish;
>   we engaged in endless work and
>   hopeless productivity,
>   and we remained hungry for real bread instead
>   of such pretend bread.
> But the poet offered otherwise: free bread,
> free water, free milk,
>   all gifts, "sent from heaven above."

III

Our mouths and our bodies are filled with bread talk,
> Of Pharaoh's bread,
> Of bread from heaven,
> Of bread from the earth via wheat,
> Of bread that does not satisfy,
> Of bread that is free . . . and abundant!

IV

Then he came. His mother had anticipated:
   she anticipated what God would do . . .
      fill the hungry with good things, and
      send the rich empty away (Luke 1:53).
She expected the redistribution of bread
   that would change the world
      and all its social relationships.
   He came, he taught, he fed, he healed,
      he surprised, he transformed.
And finally, he took bread;
   He said, "This is my body."
   We have long argued and wondered what he
      meant by that.
   But we Christians in the meantime
     keep receiving his awesome bread.
    We chew and sometimes
    we receive news with the bread.
          We are fed!

V

From that table of welcome,
   we dare imagine "Bread for the World."
   We dare to assert that "Loaves abound!"
   We imagine and assert
   right in the midst of hungry social reality.
We know very well
   that bread is managed by the rich and the powerful;
   that force of arms assures an unequal supply of bread,
   that greed denies others enough bread to live,

that the earth from which comes bread is being
    choked off in greed and chemicals,
that debt cuts people off from the bread supply,
    that greed and scarcity,
        self-indulgence and poverty go together,
            bonded by cheap labor.
We know this! We see this all around!
We do not blink before it . . .
    except in shame.

VI

And then, knowing and seeing and blinking in shame,
    we still dare anticipatory obedience,
        because bread is provided,
        because bread is given.
    We anticipate that God-given bread will override
        all the anxious ideologies of scarcity and greed.
    We still, like ancient disciples, talk of "no bread,"
        and then abundance wells up in our midst,
        right before our eyes,
                in neighborliness,
                in generosity,
                in hospitality,
                in valorizing "the least" among us,
right before our eyes in many forms
    from charity and kindness and soup kitchens,
    to policy and Marshall Plans of sustenance,
    of food stamps, and debt cancellation,
    and living wage.

Pharaoh taught us so well about scarcity while he
had surplus,
    and we are in process of unlearning
        the compelling lessons of Pharaoh.
    Pharaoh, it turns out,
        is contradicted by gospel abundance,
    on offer in the generosity of heaven,
    on offer in the "amber waves of grain" on earth,
    on offer at the table where all are welcome.
As the apostle queried us:
    "What do you have that you did not receive?"
      (1 Cor. 4:7).
We know the answer: "Nothing."
Because all is given, more than enough!

      —March 8, 2015, Columbia Theological Seminary

(On Reading Genesis 8:22)

The ceiling fan purrs softly
    and we are at ease like contented cats;
The air conditioner hums steadily,
    reassuring us like a Buddhist koan,
    and we fall back in comfort.
At the right time we break open a cold one
    and throw back our satisfied heads.

It is nonetheless not true that because it is summertime,
        the living is easy,
    because we are stressed enough:
      the job goes on,
      the vacation is hectic,
      the chaffing of summer schedule for the kids
        makes weary, and
      we wonder about violence and terror,
        and are swallowed up in anxiety.

You are the God who has promised
    that while the earth endures,
    seedtime and harvest,
    cold and heat,
    summer and winter shall not cease (Gen. 8:22).

So far you have been reliable,
      because we have yet heat in ample form and
        summer steadily.

But we do stay . . . for the most part, cool.
We think some about the heat,
    especially when we read of an inner-city death,
        heat unbearable,
        and an old fan that does not purr
                but electrocutes
        amid air that is not air-conditioned
                but given raw and humid.

We think some of heat,
    especially when we read of global warming,
        human causation, energy wasted,
        resources exploited;
There is heat out there . . . but the fan purrs
                and the air conditioner hums,
                and another cold one is offered us.

You are the God of cold and heat,
        the Lord of all our temperatures,
        the master of all our seasons.
Be your true self, and we will not be lukewarm,
        but hot for obedience, and
                cool in confidence.

You are the guarantor of regularity, and order,
and generativity.
Beyond our wee discomforts,
you are the God of all comfort.

Amid our summer heat, you promise cold to come.
Amid our disordered climate,
   you preside with fidelity.
We ask, in these warm sweaty days,
   for the courage to trust and obey your good order,
   for the energy to accept your gifts and your limits,
   for the passion to do our proper work
of creatureliness,
      all the while giving you praise and thanks.
      Amen.

The sky was filled with singing angels . . .
　　but now there are drones that hum,
　　　　but have no song to sing.
The earth was populated with rejoicing shepherds . . .
　　but now there is fear, greed, violence, and hate,
　　　　all toned joyless.
The road was busy with magi who knew that "fear
of the Lord" begins wisdom . . .
　　but now there is certitude in the service of control.

Drones, violence, and certitude make for a closed
bubble of death,
　　and now we wait to see if Christmas can break
　　open that bubble of death, for
　　　　new angel songs,
　　　　new joy-filled shepherds in eagerness, and
　　　　new trusting wisdom.

　　　　The drones are anonymous,
　　　　The violence is mad beyond naming,
　　　　The certitude is "objective" and belongs to no one.

But we know a name, a person, a memory,
a future, a vocation,
　　a God-bodied child.

And so the contest begins again in this noel,
　　of life to counter death,
　　of generosity to override violence,
　　of trust to outwit certitude.

The little blue *Evangelical Catechism* has it this way:
　　"Thine will I be in life and in death!
　　Grant me, O Lord, eternal salvation!"
That old pious phrasing claims all,
　and we do not want to be inconvenienced.
But yet again . . . Christmas
. . . is a massive inconvenience
　countering the bubble of self-deception,
　making all things new,
　　　new sky-songs,
　　　new earth joy,
　　　new knowing at fresh levels of trust.
So we wait . . . again!

　　　—Christmas 2012; quotation from Evangelical
Catechism *(St. Louis: Eden Publishing House, 1929).*

⌒⌒

We have heard it said that you are steadfast and faithful.
We ourselves have affirmed that you are steadfast
and faithful.
And we believe that about you!

But . . . we nevertheless know about acres
of vexation in our lives . . .
    about sadness and loss and anger and anxiety
      and fear;
    we know about being abandoned without help
      or hope or resources.
We pray our vexation back to you,
    because we have been told that it is all our fault,
      our grievous fault,
             . . . because of our sin.
    Except that we are not "chiefs of sinners";
      At most we specialize in trivial and incidental sins.
We pray our vexation back to you,
    because this world is with devils filled,
    with dangerous agents of evil who will us trouble.
    We know all about
      gossips who slander us,
      and bankers who exploit us,
      and preachers who lie to us,
      and merchants who cut corners on us,
      and doctors who do not pay attention to us,
      and real estate agents who betray us,
      and parents who abuse,
      and terrorists who stop at nothing,
      and academics who traffic in pretense.

The list goes on and on
and we find ourselves weak and impotent in
the face of such double-dealing.
But after our small sins and these agents of evil,
We pray our vexations back to you,
because we do not doubt that you are the major,
defining player in our lives.
We count on you and come up short;
We turn to you, and get no answer;
We know about your absence and your neglect,
and your listless inattentiveness to us,
and we are exhausted with you.
So now; listen up!
Take an inventory of our loss and hurt
and sadness and anger;
Come into this abyss of silence,
and show yourself with power and compassion.
We are ready for better than it is among us.
But it is up to you . . . Pay attention! Amen.

—*September 26, 2012, St. Timothy Episcopal Church,
Cincinnati, Ohio*

In your presence, God of all truth,
   we acknowledge that we have
      a limitless capacity for self-deception.

   We imagine that our strength will make us safe;
   we suspect that our stuff will make us happy;
   we wishfully hope that our morality
              will leave us qualified.

  We know better on a good day,
    but still we imagine and suspect and wish.

And then we are caught up short
  by your looming truth . . .
     Your sovereign power that treats
              our pride as a joke . . .
     Your deep compassion that sees through
              our little generosity . . .
     Your faithful staying power that marks
              our fickle betrayals.

We know our shabbiness because of your splendor,
  and have no resort, finally,
    except to cast our lot with you,
    to throw ourselves on your goodness,
    and to wait for your goodness to work us new.

You sovereign, compassionate, faithful one,
 be like a moth and eat through our despair . . .
 Be like a thief and rob us of our denial.
Be your true self that we — before you —
  may be our true selves . . .
   free of illusion,
   past our denial,
   buoyant beyond despair,
 ready for freedom and joy
  that comes as demanding obedience.
We pray in the name of the one who is the truth,
 the life, and the way,
  even Jesus. Amen.

* — July 25, 2007, Columbia Theological Seminary*
* Continuing Education Event*

(On Reading Exodus 20:8–11)

From the outset you called the world "very good"!
Unlike you, we find the world a dangerous,
demanding locus for our lives:
    We are beset by fears of scarcity and running out.
    We are visited by fears of falling behind
      and not measuring up.
    We are occupied with rumors of war, danger,
      and terror.
    We are frantic to protect our little places
      of well-being.
    We are weary of achieving and accomplishing.
    We are exhausted with neighbors who seem to us
      like competitors and threats.
In our anxiety we find the world at best bearable,
but less than "very good."

You, creator of heaven and earth!!
    You are so unlike us!
You do the orderly proper business of creation, of
    seedtime and harvest,
    cold and heat,
    summer and winter,
    day and night.
You sustain the regularity of seasons, sun, moon,
stars, and wind.

And then you pause in confidence:
   sure that the world will hold,
      unworried about scarcity,
         certain about flourishing,
            unbothered about the threat of chaos.
We imagine you peaceable,
cherishing your good world, at leisure,
   not restless, anxious, or worried.

We are so unlike you in our anxiety and fatigue.
We resolve, nevertheless, in your presence,
   to be more like you,
   to imitate you,
   to fall back into quiet confidence and serenity.
Like you, we may trust that your world will hold.
Like you, we may enjoy the good order of your creation.
Like you, we may be at rest and unanxious.
We are so unlike you; and you are so unlike us.
And now, in this moment of honesty before you,
   we promise to replicate your restfulness,
   finding ourselves able to bask
   in your reliable goodness,
      unanxious, unafraid, unbothered, unworried,
        defined by your durable goodness. Amen.

(Leviticus)

We assign to you three times,
  "Holy, Holy, Holy."

We do so with trepidation and
    would gladly trade your holiness
        for your gracious compassion.
    More than that, we dare claim for ourselves
    . . . with the same trepidation . . .
            or with some arrogant self-regard . . .
    The term "holy" . . .
        holy catholic church.
    We dare to imagine that as
        "royal priesthood,
        holy nation,
        God's own people" . . .
    We are somehow a match for you.

And yet in the very utterance, we cringe:
    we cringe because we know better.
    We cringe because we are too much enmeshed in
        the culture around us.

        Too much greedy economics,
        Too much predatory sexuality,
        Too much violence for neighbor,
            and violation of creation.

We cringe because we are too starchy
in our distinctiveness,
>   too sure,
>   too settled,
>   too upright.
We cringe at our holy label,
> and only late recall
>> that our holiness is not an earned adjective;
> it is rather an assigned adjective,
>>>   a gift,
>>>   a summons,
>>>   a hope,
>>>   an assurance.

All from you!

Hear our pledge at the beginning of the day,
> A vow to live into our assigned adjective,
>> Lived back to you,
>> You whom we know to be "Holy, Holy, Holy."
>>> Amen.

— October 29, 2008, Columbia Theological Seminary
DMin Day 8

(On Reading Deuteronomy 5:12–15)

We remember the old harsh days of master and slave;
    some were ruthless, demanding, unforgiving,
    others (most of us!)
    were fated to urgent performance.
But then you vetoed those presumed arrangements
    when we walked through the waters of freedom
    and we found ourselves with no commandment
        but to love neighbor.
We know now, in our own experience,
that it takes a neighborhood to make a life.

We could not, however, sustain that alternative.
We fell back to old patterns.
    Some of us became slaves again:
        some ended in hopeless debt;
        some in bondage to addictions
        that came to define us;
        some frozen in deathly emotions;
        some enlisted into the rat race that we cannot win.
Some of us, by luck or by hustle or by blessing,
became masters:
    we made money and could leverage others;
    we gained property and with it clout;
    we earned pedigrees and came out on top;
    we got credentials that entitle us to more;
    we outmatched our fellows
        and came to command them.

Without notice, we have returned to the old grind of
     master and slave,
          brick quotas and hostility and
               exploitation and alienation.
It all happened without notice;
     we find ourselves recruited in a hopeless,
     graceless contest of greed.
You, however, call us back to neighbor.
     You put in front of us our hired help, the worker
          class, the service industry, immigrants,
     the hopeless poor.
          They are so unlike us who manage and
          administer and control.
Except that in your emancipatory presence,
they are so like us,
     entitled to rest,
          assigned to dignity,
               assured of viability,
                    intended for security.
They are like us, permitted rest and leisure,
     respect and well-being.
We are on the way from master-slave to neighbor.
It is not an easy way, and we go there reluctantly.
     But we go there because of you.
          You are our first Good Neighbor.
          And you intend us all to be good neighbors,
               not on top of the heap to feather our nest
               (or nest egg),
               not at the bottom of the pile to grovel in despair.
But neighbor, in bondage only to mercy,
     compassion, justice, and generosity.
Give us courage to be on this journey together. Amen.

Our ears tingle in dismay,
Our lips quiver in bewilderment,
Our eyes blink in disbelief,
Our bodies flinch in anxiety.
We had it all arranged as we thought best.
  And then, in an inkling, we watched it go . . .
    We watched the holy city and its priesthood
      defeated;
    we watched the fortress and the armory turn
      weak in fear;
    we watched the body bleed a long, gray Friday;
    we watched our treasured world pass.
We find ourselves helpless,
      surely not our fault,
      surely not your doing,
      surely not to be explained too easily,
      not accepted too readily.
We find ourselves left void,

                    without the familiar,
                    beyond the reassuring,
                    emptied of old yeses.
And then to wait, to watch alertly,
              to grasp at straws,
              to covet hints of your rule,

watching, waiting, at the verge of Sunday, not sure,
    itching to trust,
    feeble to praise,
    tingling, but not yet congealed in despair,
    turned yet to you. Amen.

—February 19, 2002, Columbia Theological Seminary

You in our past: gracious
> steadfast,
> reliable,
> long-suffering.
You are a mouthful on the lips of our grandparents.
The hard part is you in our present,
> for after the easy violations
> we readily acknowledge
> then come the darker, hidden ones:
>> aware that appearance does not match reality;
>> aware that walk is well behind talk;
>> aware that we are enmeshed in cruelty
>>> systems well hidden but defining,
>> and we have no great yearning to be
>>> delivered from them.
Forgive us for the ways in which we are bewitched,
too settled, at ease in false places.
You in our present: gracious,
> steadfast,
> reliable,
> long-suffering.
We in the shadows asking you
> to do what you have done;
> to be whom you have been,

That we may do what we have never dared dream,
    be whom we have never imagined . . .
        free, unencumbered, unanxious,
        joyous, obedient . . .
    Yours, and not ours. Amen.

—October 3, 2001, Columbia Theological Seminary

We yearn, in every season, for your presence;
We know that our hearts will be restless,
  until they rest in you;
We are like deer who seek a watering hole
  in the drought;
We hear invitations for
"all who are weary and heavy-laden"
          (Matt. 11:28, adapted) . . .
  And approach to you seems ready and easy.
Truth to tell, we do pant restlessly,
  but not always for you.
  Sometimes, instead, for security
              or sex and beer and sports,
              or power and success,
              or beauty and acceptance
              . . . not seeking you.
Truth to tell, we know you to be no easy mark,
  with your rigorous entrance requirements
    of blamelessness, truth-telling, no bribes,
    and all manner of neighborliness.
We yearn for you in every season,
  making you too easy, imagining you too difficult,
  bewildered and unsure until you give yourself
    concretely to us . . .
  as you have done and as you do. Amen.

—September 19, 2001, Columbia Theological Seminary

Nations rise and fall,
Empires flash and fail,
We, characteristically triumphant, now know . . .
    about threat,
        danger,
        vulnerability.
In the midst of our anxiety you promise
renewed sovereignty,
More than that, you promise new human agency,
    your promised one,
        coming soon,
        coming soon by Spirit,
        coming soon in justice and righteousness,
        coming soon for the poor and the needy,
        coming soon.
Whereby the earth dazzles,
    the animals gentle,
    the children are safe,
    and we, all of us, laugh, and love, and give thanks.
You promise and we in our cynicism scarcely listen,
    we in our fear surge in doubt,
    we in our usual control, resist.
But you promise . . . and we wait and watch,
        wait and hope,
        wait and trust, and
        wait as long as
        we must. Amen.

—October 16, 2001, Columbia Theological Seminary

We are citizens of your city,
> your place of presence
> and of promise,
> our place of well-being and security.
We name and give thanks for our many Jerusalems.
We know about the failure of our place with you,
> of hopes for justice and
> the reality of injustice,
> of promises of fidelity
> and our bent toward
> fickleness.
We know about your impatience and finally your
exhaustion with our best place,
> and the way trouble comes there,
> inchoate and wild,
> from you,
> but otherwise explained,
> otherwise explained,
> but perhaps from you.
We are citizens of our city that is not a continuing city.
And so at our best, we stand eager for "Afterward"
> after failure and after suffering,
> afterward that is your show of
> sovereign goodness,
> afterward a new haven, a new
> earth, a new home,
> a better country, a city you
> promise and give.

Give us boldness in hope,
    patience in our obedience,
    pure joy in your gift of city, and our being there
        as your people.
We pray through Jesus who is, first and last,
    our continuing city. Amen.

    —*December 5, 2001, Columbia Theological Seminary*

You are the God from whom no secret can be hid.
  You are the God who knows . . .
  You know how much we love the Lord Jesus,
    and how glad we are to be in ministry.
  You know our passion and our commitment,
    our delight in this vocation.
  You know, as well, how demanding that call is,
    how we despair and
    how we fear for ourselves and our loved ones.
  You know how deeply we resent
    groundless hostility,
    ill-informed criticism, and
    cheap shots.
  You know how we sometimes cross over the line
    in impatience and anger, and
    sometimes rage enough to will revenge
      and we live with an ethic of "getting even."
      But then we bury it as "nice people."

We also know a lot.
  We know you are the God who calls and who sends,
                who delivers and
                who commands.
  We know you are the God who has promised to
                be with us.
  We know, as well, that sometimes you are
    absent, neglectful, and indifferent,
    and we are left to our own thin resources.

We know that you have healing power,
                    but sometimes
                    withhold that power.
So we pray, bind us to you as you are bound to us.
        Be your full-time, grace-filled self toward us,
        that we in turn may be filled with joy,
                gratitude, and glad obedience.
We give you thanks for our calling,
        and are glad indeed that it is you
                who has called us. Amen.

—*October 28, 2004, Columbia Theological Seminary*

You have known, before we know,
   that we live in an ocean of fickleness and unfaith.

We are partly perpetrators of faithlessness:
      not loving you wholly,
      not loving neighbor generously,
      not caring for self gracefully,
      using up our energy on skewed ways of living.

We are partly victims of fickleness:
         double-crossed and hammered,
         betrayed and misrepresented,
      even by those close at hand,
      even by good church people,
      even by you on your bad days
         when you do not show up.

We are perpetrators and victims of infidelity
         and left by it exhausted and
                     anxious,
         zealous to make it work,
         in despair that it ever can.

Victims and perpetrators, perpetrators and victims,
    and we wait . . .
        We wait for the other shoe to fall;
        but beyond both shoes we wait for you,
            for your signs of promise,
            for your word of care,
            for your bread broken,
            for your wine blessed and poured out.

We wait for nothing less than newness
        that overrides our shabbiness;
    and we know it is only from you that we may
        begin again.

This day, this very day,
        call into existence that which does not exist;
        call into existence a fresh
            dimension of your coming kingdom,
        and make us, as we are not in this instant,
            glad participants in your new regime.

Death will be all right for us when it comes.
    But dying is another matter . . .
        so slow,
        so painful,
        so humiliating.

Death will be a quick turn,
        the winking of an eye,
    but dying turns and twists and waits and teases.

We have not died;
    but we know about dying:
        We watch the inching pain of cancer,
                the oozing ache of alienation,
                the tears of stored-up hurt.

    We can smell the dying,
        of bombs and shells
        of direct hit and
            collateral damage,
        of napalm spread thin and even,
        of orange that waits years to show,
        of cities turned craters
            and lives to empty stares.

We watch close or distant;
    we brace and stiffen
        and grow cynical or uncaring.

And death wins . . .
    we, robbed of vitality,
        brought low by failed hope,
                    lost innocence,
                    emptied childhood,
                    and stillness.

    We keep going . . . but barely;
    We gather at the grave,
      watching the sting and
            the victory of dread.

We confess with our mothers and our fathers
that the only real power in our lives comes from
the speaking of your word to us.

Yet we find ourselves, day by day,
to be but weak, frail, and fragile.

We are in the midst of a weak and frail and
fragile people who yearn for power and know
powerlessness.

We thank you for the mystery
of Jesus of Nazareth,
by whom we know that weakness becomes power,
foolishness becomes wisdom, and
poverty becomes wealth.
Our frailty, foolishness, and poverty
are transformed
into strength, wisdom, and well-being
by trusting ourselves to you.

So, at the beginning of this day and the
beginning of this week, we submit ourselves
to your mercy.

We pray that the power of your Spirit
may come upon us and upon your whole church,
that we may name with joy and passion
    the name of Jesus over our lives.

Amen.

—October 11, 1976

(On Reading Psalm 77)

How great thou art!
    Except you do not seem so great or big or
    dominant in a world coming unglued.
We say, "Surely goodness and mercy will follow me
all the days of my life."
    But I find myself pursued, rather, by scarcity and
        resentment and anger,
    and your steadfast love seems quite remote.
We say, "I will fear no evil, for thou art with me."
    But I do fear . . .
    I fear Ebola and terrorism and market collapse and,
    closer home, I fear losing out or being left behind or
    I fear being left out or failing or not having done
        enough,
    and you do not appear to be with me.
You are "the peace that passes all understanding,"
    But we are unsettled, ill at ease with the world
        as it is, argumentative, disturbed, restless, on
        edge.
So here we are in your presence
    with our most treasured mantras of faith:
        We say them passionately and believe them.
        We recite them by rote
           and do not pay attention to them,
        We say them but know better.

The subtext of our lives tells otherwise:
    Other than "How great thou art";
    Other than "steadfast love will follow me";
    Other than "I will fear no evil";
    Other than "the peace that passes
      all understanding."
Here we are in your presence
before whom no secret can be hid,
    with our mantras of trust
    and our lives of disease.
We can only present ourselves as we are before you,
    trusting and ill at ease,
    hoping but unsure,
    yearning, but resisting.
Here we are . . .
        we have no other place . . .
                so here we are.
                Amen.

*—October 15, 2014, St. Timothy Episcopal Church,
Cincinnati, Ohio*

(On Reading Psalm 35)

We have not yet arrived at your promised shalom;
We have not yet gotten entry into
your promised kingdom.
    So we must pray in the meantime,
    We must pray to you from our circumstance.
    And our circumstance is most often one of worry,
    need, and anxiety,
        Too much pressure,
        Too many demands,
        Too many risks.
We are pressed on every side
    With demands
        On our time,
        On our energy,
        On our money.
    So many voices that keep insisting and asking
    and wanting and needing.
We are recruited by too many voices:
    Join this,
    Attend to that,
    Help us out.
    Those voices that keep summoning us
    and dispatching us.
We are situated in too many risks,
    Of money running short,
    Of violence too immediate,
    Of a din of threats,

Of medical worry . . . be this and do that
   . . . until we are exhausted, and it's only Wednesday.
We are surrounded by voices of threat, seduction, demand,
   and what we long for is your voice,
   your presence,
   your gracious welcome,
   your steadfast assurance.
So here is what you might speak to us:
   I am your salvation;
   I am with you always;
   Do not fear,
   I have heard your cry.
   Taste and see how good the Lord is.
Say that to us!
   And then give us good ears to hear,
   give us good tongues to speak back to you,
   give us quiet hearts in the midst of the din;
   give us patience to receive as you give;
   give us impatience to insist against you.
In our neediness, give us good hearts that we may,
soon and late, in dark and in light,
find the freedom and energy and courage
to say with our whole selves,
   Hallelujah,
   Hallelujah,
   Hallelujah! Amen.

   —*October 29, 2014, St. Timothy Episcopal Church,*
   Cincinnati, Ohio